THE
AMERICAN
GOVERNORSHIP

Coleman B. Ransone, Jr.

THE AMERICAN GOVERNORSHIP

CONTRIBUTIONS IN POLITICAL SCIENCE, NUMBER 69

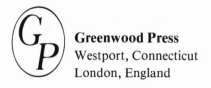

Greenwood Press
Westport, Connecticut
London, England

Library of Congress Cataloging in Publication Data

Ransone, Coleman Bernard, 1920–
    The American governorship.

    (Contributions in political science, ISSN 0147-1066;
no. 69)
    Bibliography: p.
    Includes index.
    1. Governors—United States.   I. Title.   II. Series.

JK2447.R29   353.9'131   81-6653
ISBN 0-313-22977-5 (lib. bdg.)   AACR2

Library of Congress Catalog Card Number: 81-6653
ISBN: 0-313-22977-5
ISSN: 0147-1066

First published in 1982

Greenwood Press
A division of Congressional Information Service, Inc.
88 Post Road West, Westport, Connecticut 06881

Printed in the United States of America

10 9 8 7 6 5 4 3 2 1

In memory of my father and mother
Coleman and Natalie Ransone

CONTENTS

TABLES

ACKNOWLEDGMENTS

At the very outset of this volume I wish to acknowledge my debt to the University of Alabama Press for its generous permission to use some of the concepts, language, and data from my earlier study, *The Office of Governor in the United States,* copyrighted in 1956 by the University of Alabama Press. The current study is essentially a comparison of the governor's functions in the fifties with his functions in the seventies. Consequently, much of the material on the governor's functions in the fifties comes from the earlier study.

A grant from the Research Grants Committee of the University of Alabama made possible my second round of interviews in thirteen states in 1976. Consequently, a debt of gratitude is owed to the committee for making these interviews possible.

In addition to the University of Alabama Press and the Research Grants Committee, I would like to acknowledge the work of four research assistants at the University of Alabama. Each of these served at different periods during the three years in which the book was written. These junior colleagues—Digambar Mishra, Thom Simpson, Tommy Patrick, and Dana Stone—did much of the detailed work necessary to prepare the tables in the study. The system used in ranking the states in terms of party control in Chapter 1 was the result of a suggestion made by Thom Simpson when we worked on the tables for that chapter.

Finally, I would like to acknowledge a special debt to Jean D. Rosene. She not only typed and proofread the manuscript but in the process translated my handwriting into English and quietly corrected my more glaring errors in spelling.

Needless to say, nothing in these acknowledgments should be interpreted as an attempt to shift the blame for any errors either in fact or interpretation. Where such errors exist, they belong entirely to me.

Coleman B. Ransone, Jr.
Tuscaloosa, Alabama

INTRODUCTION

My last major work on the role of the state governor was *The Office of Governor in the United States,* published in 1956. This book was based primarily on interviews with governors, members of the governors' staffs, department heads, legislators, capitol correspondents, and other persons knowledgeable about state government. A major finding of that study was that the governor's functions consisted primarily of three areas of operations—public relations, policy formation, and management. Of these, policy formation was the most significant and public relations the most time-consuming. Management came in third both in significance and in the time devoted to it by the governors.

The study reported on in this book is based on the same general methodology used in 1956. It, too, relies heavily on interviews in selected states. These interviews were conducted in the fall of 1976. In addition, a good deal has been written on the governorship in the intervening twenty years, and these books and articles also were consulted in preparing the current study. The primary purpose of this book is to determine whether or not the governor's functions changed in the twenty years between the first study in 1956 and the second study in 1976. In short, did the governors of the seventies have the same functions as the governors of the fifties, and did they place the same emphasis on various aspects of their functions as did their counterparts some twenty years earlier? This question underlies the discussion of the governor's functions throughout this book but is specifically addressed in the last chapter where the present and future role of the governor is examined.

The first four chapters of the book consider certain other factors that are vital in arriving at an answer to this question. A governor does not operate in a vacuum, and what he does and how he does it are influenced by various ecological factors. The most important of these factors are considered in Chapter 1. They include the impact of the party on the governorship, the governor's role in intergovernmental relations, and his formal powers—his term of office, his appointing power, and his salary as it affects performance.

The second chapter is concerned with the problems involved in being elected governor. In particular, it focuses on what it costs to run successfully for the governorship. It also takes a look at some of the fascinating campaign techniques that have been developed in the constant search for new methods of reaching and persuading voters. Among these methods, the one that has grown most since the fifties is the use of television. This medium is apparently effective but is an exceedingly expensive way to appeal to voters.

Chapter 3 returns to the central thesis of the study. It compares the governor's functions in the 1950s with those in the 1970s. This comparison is made primarily from two perspectives. First, several studies of the time spent by the governor on various aspects of his duties in the fifties are compared to similar studies in the seventies. Second, the governors' own views of the executive function are summarized. These views are taken primarily from interviews, articles, or speeches by governors. Again, a comparison is made between the views of the governors in the fifties and in the seventies.

One of the conclusions reached in Chapter 3 is that policy formation in the seventies, as in the fifties, was the most significant of the governor's functions. Consequently, this role is examined in more depth in Chapter 4. Here the governor's role in policy formation is considered, beginning with the development of policy and plans for a legislative program and ending with a consideration of the nature of executive-legislative relations and the methods used by the governor in influencing legislation.

As noted at the beginning of this section, the final chapter is a summary of the findings on the governor's functions in the fifties as compared to the seventies. It also attempts a few predictions as to how the governorship in the eighties may develop. This is an interesting but risky enterprise in view of the changes that have already been found in the seventies as compared to the fifties.

THE
AMERICAN
GOVERNORSHIP

1

THE CHANGING PATTERN OF GUBERNATORIAL POLITICS

During the last thirty years the American governor has emerged as a policy leader of no mean proportions. He also is emerging gradually as a leader in terms of more recently gained powers in the field of state management. His office has become the primary center of public attention at the state level, and his actions and speeches have considerable influence in molding public opinion. This tendency toward a strong governor means that the office has increased in importance; in most states the governor is one of the key people in the fascinating game of political chess. It is now of crucial importance to each state party to elect its candidate as governor and of considerable importance to each national party as well. Furthermore, the citizens of a state have an important stake in the governorship because the governor's increased power and importance strengthen his ability to take action that can affect their lives.

The American state has not been displaced as a unit of government. Its role has been altered by increasing federal participation in fields formerly thought to be reserved for the states, but the importance of the states has been enhanced, not diminished, by the federal government's programs as they are carried out in practice. While it is undeniable that the federal government has assumed new powers and functions, this is also true of the states. The governor, as the chief figure on the state political scene, has assumed increased importance as a result of these federally financed, state-administered programs.

In order to understand the functions of the modern American governor, it is necessary to understand the legal and political environment in which he operates. While this environment has many facets, it will be considered in this chapter under three major headings—the governor and party control, the governor's role in intergovernmental relations, and the governor's formal powers.

The Governor and Party Control

The idea of classifying states on the basis of certain criteria into rough political groupings has a long and honorable tradition in the study of politics. Perhaps V. O. Key as much as any recent scholar was responsible for focusing attention on such classifications. They have indeed flourished, and the number of classifications as well as classifiers is now legion. As the student of state politics is well aware, these classifications vary considerably depending upon the classifier. For example, it would not be unusual to find a given state classified by one scholar as "one-party Democratic," by another as "two-party, leaning Democratic," and by a third as a definite "two-party" state. These apparent discrepancies generally arise for two reasons. First, the criteria used by each author may be different, and second, the time periods being studied may not be the same.

To take a simple example of the criteria problem, it may be entirely logical to classify a state as "one-party Democratic" if the classification is based only on state elections. Thus, if one party controlled both the governorship and both houses of the legislature over an entire ten-year period, the state may legitimately be called "one-party" for that period. However, the same state may suddenly become "leaning Democratic" if the presidential races over the same ten-year period also are considered. If the state went Republican in the presidential race just preceding the period and in one of the two presidential elections during this period, it may legitimately be considered to have lost some of its Democratic solidarity. In addition, if other federal races are considered, such as congressional elections, the original Democratic classification may become even less valid. For example, if a majority of the members of the house and perhaps one senator were Republican during this period, the Democratic nature of the state may be more closely questioned. If these elections are given considerable weight, the state legitimately may be shifted to "two-party" status.

The same line of reasoning applies to time periods. For those students of politics who have followed the political fortunes of the two major parties at the state level over the last thirty years, it comes as something of a shock that even at the state level there is no longer a "solid" Republican state to be found. Even if the same criteria are used, the states shift from one category to another not only over a time span of thirty years but also from one ten-year period to the next and even from election to election. Some of these shifts are illustrated in the next section in Tables 1, 2, 3, and 4, which emphasize the time factor.

Thus the classifications in the next section are presented only as snapshots of the party situation at given ten-year intervals. Political classifications are very tenuous and change under the impact of local or national pressures. Consequently, it should be emphasized that the classifications that follow have been made in retrospect over the period from 1930 to 1980. Some of the classifications even of the period 1971–80 probably will not apply with equal force to the political situation existing when this book is released, since it appears that some of the states are again in the process of change. The classifications certainly should not be taken as a prediction of future state political trends. The purpose of these classifications is to form a background for the later discussion of the functions of the governor, particularly his role in policy formation. It is well to remember that all political classifications are not only the children of criteria but are also the nieces and nephews of the time warp; hence they are to be regarded as useful but very suspect in their long-range accuracy.

A Political Typology of the States

For the purposes of this study each of the states is classified as being either one-party Democratic, normally Democratic, two-party, normally Republican, or one-party Republican. This classification is shown on a state-by-state basis in Tables 2, 3, and 4 for each ten-year period from 1951 through 1980 and is summarized in Table 1 for the entire thirty-year span. The assignment of states to a particular category was based on two criteria—party control of the governorship and party control of the legislature. Party control of the governorship was determined on a year-by-year basis by determining the party to which the governor belonged for the periods 1951–60, 1961–70, and 1971–80. Party control of the legislature also was calculated for each house for each year during these periods. Control of a house was awarded to the party that had a simple majority of the seats in that house. The fact that the governor's party has a majority in a house does not mean that the house will automatically vote for the governor's bills, but it does suggest that his party will organize the legislature and control the flow of business. While there is no proven percentage of seats that guarantees party regularity, it has been suggested by Sarah McCally Morehouse that the governor is most likely to succeed in securing the passage of his legislative program when his party does not have an overwhelming majority in each house. She points out that it is an advantage to the governor for his party to have a majority so that it can organize the legislature. "However, extra seats over a comfortable majority appear to be a disadvantage to him. As the proportion of his party of seats in the legislature rises, rivalries are generated which the governor cannot afford. Gubernatorial support falls as the size of his majority increases."[1]

TABLE 1
INDEX OF PARTY CONTROL: THE GOVERNOR AND THE LEGISLATURE, 1951–1980

Time Period	One-Party Democratic (1.00)	Normally Democratic (1.01–1.67)	Two-Party (1.68–2.32)	Normally Republican (2.33–2.99)	One-Party Republican (3.00)
1951–60	13	4	13	13	3
1961–70	8	14	14	10	2
1971–80	10	17	17	4	0

SOURCES: Tables 2, 3, and 4.

NOTE: Minnesota and Nebraska have been omitted from this table. See the notes in Tables 2, 3, and 4 on the generally nonpartisan character of their elections.

TABLE 2
INDEX OF PARTY CONTROL: THE GOVERNOR AND THE LEGISLATURE, 1951-1960

One-Party Democratic		Normally Democratic		Two-Party		Normally Republican		One-Party Republican	
Alabama	1.00	Missouri	1.10	New Mexico	1.70	Oregon	2.45	New Hampshire	3.00
Arkansas	1.00	West Virgina	1.40	Maryland	1.80	California	2.55	North Dakota	3.00
Florida	1.00	Rhode Island	1.50	Massachusetts	1.90	New York	2.60	Vermont	3.00
Georgia	1.00	Arizona	1.60	Washington	1.90	Maine	2.60		
Kentucky	1.00			Michigan	1.95	Iowa	2.60		
Louisiana	1.00			Colorado	2.00	Kansas	2.60		
Mississippi	1.00			Connecticut	2.00	Indiana	2.70		
N. Carolina	1.00			Ohio	2.00	Illinois	2.70		
Oklahoma	1.00			Delaware	2.10	Idaho	2.70		
S. Carolina	1.00			Pennsylvania	2.20	South Dakota	2.70		
Tennessee	1.00			New Jersey	2.25	Wisconsin	2.70		
Texas	1.00			Montana	2.30	Wyoming	2.70		
Virginia	1.00			Nevada	2.30	Utah	2.75		

SOURCES: *The Book of the States*, volumes for 1950–51 through 1960–61 (Lexington, Ky.: Council of State Governments, 1950, 1952, 1954, 1956, 1958, 1960).

NOTE: Minnesota and Nebraska had a nonpartisan legislature and are omitted from the table. Alaska and Hawaii had not yet been admitted to the Union.

TABLE 3
INDEX OF PARTY CONTROL: THE GOVERNOR AND THE LEGISLATURE, 1961–1970

One-Party Democratic		Normally Democratic		Two-Party		Normally Republican		One-Party Republican	
Alabama	1.00	Tennessee	1.05	Alaska	1.75	Pennsylvania	2.35	Idaho	3.00
Georgia	1.00	Virginia	1.10	Nevada	1.75	Maine	2.40	South Dakota	3.00
Louisiana	1.00	West Virginia	1.20	Massachusetts	1.80	Vermont	2.40		
Mississippi	1.00	Hawaii	1.30	Oklahoma	1.80	Wisconsin	2.50		
Missouri	1.00	Connecticut	1.30	Washington	1.80	Michigan	2.50		
N. Carolina	1.00	Kentucky	1.30	Indiana	1.85	Colorado	2.50		
S. Carolina	1.00	Maryland	1.40	North Dakota	1.90	Kansas	2.60		
Texas	1.00	Arkansas	1.40	Utah	2.00	New York	2.70		
		Florida	1.40	Iowa	2.10	Wyoming	2.70		
		Delaware	1.55	Illinois	2.10	Ohio	2.75		
		California	1.60	Arizona	2.20				
		New Mexico	1.60	Montana	2.20				
		Rhode Island	1.60	New Hampshire	2.30				
		New Jersey	1.65	Oregon	2.30				

SOURCES: *The Book of the States*, volumes for 1960–61 through 1970–71 (Lexington, Ky.: Council of State Governments, 1960, 1962, 1964, 1966, 1968, 1970).

NOTE: Minnesota and Nebraska had a nonpartisan legislature and are omitted from the table.

8

TABLE 4
INDEX OF PARTY CONTROL: THE GOVERNOR AND THE LEGISLATURE, 1971–1980

One-Party Democratic		Normally Democratic		Two-Party		Normally Republican		One-Party Republican
Alabama	1.00	Kentucky	1.10	Oregon	1.70	Vermont	2.50	None
Arkansas	1.00	Louisiana	1.10	Washington	1.75	Iowa	2.60	
Florida	1.00	Montana	1.15	Alaska	1.85	New Hampshire	2.65	
Georgia	1.00	Texas	1.20	Maine	1.90[a]	Indiana	2.80	
Hawaii	1.00	Nevada	1.30	Ohio	1.90			
Maryland	1.00	Wisconsin	1.40	South Dakota	1.95			
Mississippi	1.00	California	1.40	North Dakota	1.95			
New Mexico	1.00	Massachusetts	1.40	Delaware	2.00			
Oklahoma	1.00	N. Carolina	1.40	Illinois	2.00			
Rhode Island	1.00	S. Carolina	1.40	Idaho	2.00			
		Pennsylvania	1.40	Virginia	2.00			
		Missouri	1.40	New York	2.10			
		New Jersey	1.50	Michigan	2.10			
		Utah	1.60	Arizona	2.20			
		Connecticut	1.60	Colorado	2.30			
		Tennessee	1.60	Kansas	2.30			
		West Virginia	1.60	Wyoming	2.35			

SOURCES: *The Book of the States*, volumes for 1970–71 through 1980–81 (Lexington, Ky.: Council of State Governments, 1970, 1972, 1974, 1976, 1978, 1980).

NOTE: During this period Nebraska had a nonpartisan legislature. Minnesota had a Democratic Farmer-Labor governor in 1971–78 and a Republican in 1979–80. Prior to 1972 Minnesota had a nonpartisan legislature. After 1972 both House and Senate were Democratic except in 1979–80 when the House was evenly divided and the Senate Democratic. Both Nebraska and Minnesota are omitted from the table above.

[a]Maine had an Independent governor from 1975 to 1978 but a Democratic governor for the remainder of the period. Since the Senate was Republican during the entire period and the House Republican, 1971–74, but Democratic in 1975–80, Maine is considered to be a competitive state.

9

There were no three periods over the last thirty years for which the data would be entirely comparable if the governor's term were used as a unit of measurement. Because the governor and the legislature are elected for different periods in some states, their terms are not necessarily coterminous. For example, some legislatures have four-year terms for both houses that are coterminous with that of governor; some have two-year terms for the house but four-year terms for the senate; and in some states there are systems of elections under which senators have staggered terms, but members of the house are all elected at the same time. Thus, it is difficult to ascertain exactly the situation prevailing throughout a governor's term of office, since it may change at least every two years in some states. For this reason the data were calculated on a year-by-year basis, so that what is actually being measured is the number of years in a given period in which one party either did or did not control the governorship and either did or did not have a majority in one or both houses of the legislature.

In order to compare party control over a period of time within a state and to compare party control among states, some simple mathematical statement had to be found that would express a situation such as divided control in which one party controls the governorship but another the legislature, but that would also cover the more traditional situation in which the governor and the legislature were of the same party. The statement also had to be flexible enough to take into consideration more complex situations in which the governor and one house of the legislature were of one party and the other house was controlled by the opposing party. In addition, the formula had to be stated in such a way that the reader could determine whether such power belonged to the Republicans or the Democrats.

This translation of party control into an easily recognized number was accomplished by ranking each state for each year in the period under consideration on a scale from 1.00 (Democratic) to 3.00 (Republican). A ranking of 1.00 is assigned to the governorship, to the house, or to the senate when it is controlled by the Democratic party. A ranking of 3.00 is assigned to the governorship, to the house, or to the senate when it is under Republican control. These figures are then multiplied by their assigned weights (2 for the governor and 1 each for the senate and house) and added together to get a total for any given year. The formula used above in determining party control gives equal weight to both the governor and the legislature. Each house of that body is given a weight of 1, for a total weight of 2 for the legislature. The justification for giving equal weight to each of these branches of state government lies in the assumption that they are coequal partners in the determination of public policy, at least as that policy is expressed in legislation.

Any state would serve as a good example of the application of this formula to the actual political situation in a given year. However, since the state of Oregon is subject to the kind of change we would expect in a two-party state, it will serve as a good illustration of how the calculations were made. Oregon has a four-year term for the governor, a four-year term for the senate, and a two-year term for the house. Consequently, the senate will generally stay under the control of one party for four years, although it may shift at the end of each four-year period. The house, on the other hand, can, and does, sometimes change in the middle of the governor's term.

For example, during the first four years of the 1970s Tom Mc-Call (Republican) was the governor of Oregon. The senate was controlled by the Democrats and the house was under Republican control for the first two years (1971-72), but the house switched to Democratic control for 1973-74. The score for 1971 thus was calculated as follows: governor (R) = $3.00 \times 2 = 6.00$; senate (D) = $1.00 \times 1 = 1.00$; and house (R) = $3.00 \times 1 = 3.00$; or $6.00 + 1.00 + 3.00 = 10.00 \div 4 = 2.50$. Each of the years of the decade was calculated in the same manner. In 1972 the score remained 2.50, since there was no change in party control. However, in 1973 the score changed to 2.00 as a result of a shift in the house, which came under Democratic control. The same situation prevailed in 1974 with a Republican governor but a Democratic senate and house for the same 2.00 control figure.

In the election of 1974 a Democrat, Robert W. Straub, was elected governor. The senate remained Democratic after the 1974 election as did the house after both the 1974 and the 1976 elections. Thus, in 1975 the score shifted to a solid 1.00. This 1.00 was the result of a Democratic governor (2.00) plus a Democratic senate (1.00) plus a Democratic house (1.00), or $2.00 + 1.00 + 1.00 = 4.00 \div 4 = 1.00$. This situation prevailed for four years—1975,

1976, 1977, and 1978. However, in the 1978 election Victor Atiyeh (Republican) was elected governor, although both the house and senate remained Democratic. Thus, the state's party control score for 1979 and 1980 was again 2.00.

For the decade the score thus read: 2.50 (1971–72) + 2.00 (1973–74) + 1.00 (1975–76–77–78) + 2.00 (1979–80) or 17.00 ÷ 10 = 1.70. This is the score for Oregon used in Table 4 for the period 1971–80.

Each of the figures above gives us a reasonable clue as to party control year-by-year in Oregon. In addition, the 1.70 ranking puts Oregon in the two-party category for 1971–80 in comparison with other states on the question of party control of the governorship and the legislature.

The same kind of calculations were made for each of the states for the last thirty years and are shown grouped by decades in Tables 2, 3, and 4. In addition, Table 1 gives a summary of the shifts in party control over time. These tables show quite clearly that party control (as was the case in Oregon) may shift from one governor's term to the next or even within one governor's term if one house of the legislature has only a two-year term. The ten-year tables give a broad-brush treatment to party control by state and by decade, while Table 1 clearly shows the ebb and flow of party control for the states as a whole. However, it should be remembered that what the figures in Tables 1, 2, 3, and 4 show is only the general political configuration of the state based on party control of the governorship and the legislature. While the control figures are useful, they should not be taken too literally. For example, the figure of 2.00 represents an evenly divided state, with one party in control of the governorship and the opposition party in control of both houses of the legislature. However, such divided control does not necessarily mean in practice what it does in theory. If the legislature voted along strictly party lines, it would support or fail to support the governor depending on his party affiliation. Thus, in theory we should have a stalemate either when a state has a Republican governor and a Democratic house and senate or has a Democratic governor and a Republican house and senate. In practice this is generally not the case, as has been demonstrated over the years by astute governors who have, in practice, been able to work with legislatures that are completely controlled by the opposite party. When there is divided control in its less extreme form, in which the governor has one house under the control of his party, he is frequently able to get much of his program through the legislature in spite of the opposition party's control of the other house. Therefore, while these calculations produce numbers that can be used as a shorthand method of suggesting party control, the number used for a given state should not be confused with the actual control by the party as opposed to potential control.

All that these figures show is a comparison of the states based on party control of the legislature and the governorship. The party control of these two branches of government appears to be among those factors which make the greatest difference in state politics and policymaking. If the governor and both houses of the legislature are Democratic, this appears to be a more significant fact about the politics of a state in a given year than the fact that the state's two United States senators are Republican. Ticket splitting in state politics seems to be happening more frequently in recent years as the voters separate national from state politics and vote for one party for the president or for the United States Senate or House, and for another party for the state legislature or the governor. Thus, when discussing politics at the state level, the most important elections to be analyzed are those of the governor and the legislature. The classification system described in this section gives a rough, overall idea of party control as far as the governor and the legislature are concerned. However, simply because these classifications have been translated into mathematical terms, they should not be allowed to give an illusion of an exactitude which does not exist in politics.

The calculations were rerun using a formula that gave the governor a weight of 1 and each house of the legislature a weight of 1. In the case of Oregon in the period 1971–80, the score would change to 1.53 and would move Oregon into the normally Democratic category. This shift reflects primarily the fact that the senate was Democratic throughout the period and that the house was Democratic for eight years of the ten-year period. The problem then becomes a matter of judgment as to which figure, 1.70 or 1.53, best reflects party control in Oregon during the period. The author is of the opinion that the first formula is the better of the two in reflecting the question of party control since it put Oregon (though at the Democratic end of the scale) in the two-party category.

However, the shifts caused by using the second formula instead of the first are not significant. For example, in none of the three decades do any states shift more than one category and the largest number of states that shifted during any decade was five. In the 1971–80 period, there were four states that shifted categories. The normally Democratic group lost one state (Utah), which moved into the two-party group. However, the normally Democratic group gained two states (Washington and Oregon), which shifted from the two-party to the normally Democratic column by a very slim margin. The normally Republican group, already low at four states, lost Iowa, which shifted to the two-party designation.

Overall, the shift of four states in the seventies, five in the sixties, and four in the fifties did not seem of enough significance to warrant the substitution of the second formula for the first formula in determining the categories for this study. Consequently, the first formula as described above in the Oregon example was that used as a basis for Tables 1, 2, 3, and 4.

Table 1 illustrates, sometimes dramatically, the shift in fortunes of the Democratic and Republican parties at the state level. For example, the solidly Democratic states dropped from thirteen in the period 1951–60 to eight in the period 1961–70, because of Republican inroads in the control of the governorship in previously Democratic states. However, the Democrats made a minor comeback in the seventies with ten states showing Democratic control not only of the governorship but also of both houses of the legislature throughout the ten-year period.

The decrease in the solidly Democratic states is reflected in the growth of the normally Democratic states. This group of states, which is sometimes classified as two-party, leaning Democratic, has grown at a rate even greater than the decline of the solidly Democratic states. While in the 1950s only four states fell in the normally Democratic category, by the 1960s the number had increased to fourteen and by the 1970s had risen to seventeen states. This rise is particularly interesting when coupled with the decline of their counterparts on the Republican side. What the figures show as far as the Republicans are concerned is a steady decline of Republicanism in the solidly Republican states; this group dropped from three in the 1950s to two in the 1960s to none in the 1970s. Gone, apparently, are the Republican bastions in New England and the Midwest. Although Republican strength is still reflected in the normally Republican states, this category declined from thirteen states in the 1950s to ten states in the 1960s and to only four states in the 1970s. This trend is almost the reverse of the growth in the normally Democratic states.

It is also possible to look at the overall picture of state politics from a slightly different perspective. One approach is to add the solidly Democratic states to the normally Democratic states and compare this figure with one obtained by adding the solidly Republican states to the normally Republican states. When this calculation is made, the trend is indeed striking. In the 1950s there were seventeen Democratic states and sixteen Republican states. However, by the 1960s the score was twenty-two Democratic states to twelve Republican states which in the 1970s increased to a twenty-seven to four advantage. Thus, it is quite clear that in terms of party control of the governorship and the legislature, there has been a steady movement toward the Democratic end of the political spectrum.

In the meantime, the two-party states really did not grow at the rate which might have been expected although they did increase from thirteen in the 1950s to fourteen in the 1960s and seventeen in the 1970s. However, the changes at the state level have not been in the direction of a highly competitive two-party system; by the end of the sixties the solidly Republican states had disappeared and did not reappear in the seventies. On the other hand, the solidly Democratic states, in decline in the sixties, made a slight comeback in the seventies. The real gain over the last thirty years, however, has been in the category of normally Democratic states, which has grown partly at the expense of the one-party Democratic states but has also sharply cut into what was previously considered to be competitive states. These shifts over time are shown in more detail in Tables 2, 3, and 4 which give the data for individual states for the periods 1951–60, 1961–70, and 1971–80.

The growth of the normally Democratic states can be explained by the fact that the Democrats have elected more governors in traditionally solidly Republican states and in normally Republican states, where they also have won control of at least one house of the legislature. It would be too strong a statement to say that the governor carried one house of the legislature with him in his victories. However, for many reasons the strength of the Democrats has grown along with their ability to capture the governorship. On the other hand, the Republicans, while they have been able to elect a series of personally popular Republican governors in what are normally Democratic states, do not seem to have been able to make substantial inroads in the Democratic control of the legislature either in the solidly Democratic states or in the normally Democratic states. It is this inability to carry at least one house of the legislature which has changed the pattern of state politics over this thirty-year period. Thus, as will be shown in the next section of this chapter, more and more Republican governors find themselves facing a Democratic house or senate and a more difficult task in implementing their programs. While Democratic governors may also face divided legislatures, they are less likely than the Republicans to have a completely unfriendly legislature because the Democrats usually have been able to capture at least one house.

Divided Party Control

As was suggested earlier in this chapter, there is no fixed percentage of seats in a legislative body that guarantees the governor's party working control of the legislature. Nevertheless, it appears logical to assume that it is to the governor's advantage to have a majority of his party in both houses of the legislature. Given this majority, the governor should more easily secure the passage of his administration's bills than if the opposition party controlled one or both houses.

However, this hypothesis, while logical and widely accepted, may not be in accord with the realities of the situation in a substantial number of states. In the first place, it is not in conformity with experience in the one-party states nor in most of the normally Democratic or Republican states. The problem is too much of a good thing, that is, the majority of the governor's party is so large (in many cases 100 percent) that a "no-party" situation exists. The governor cannot, with any realistic expectation of support, call upon all good party members to support his programs because all, or almost all, of the legislators in both houses belong to the governor's party. Hence, a governor in a one-party state finds himself in the position of being forced to build a block of votes from any source that he can in order to get his legislation passed.

As a practical matter, what any governor needs, regardless of the party situation, is enough votes to get his legislation passed. "Enough" in this context is only one vote more in favor of his bill than the votes that his opponents can muster against it. A "vote" is actually a neutral entity in that a Republican vote for the bill counts just as much as a Democratic vote. If there are 100 members of the house present and voting in a given state, what the governor needs is 51 votes for his legislation, and it makes no immediate difference if these votes are Democratic or Republican. Consequently, in examining the relationship of the governor to the legislature, we must be careful not to assume unconsciously that the textbook pattern of party control prevails. Legislative situations that appear on the surface to be diametrically opposed to one another may in practice actually represent much the same problem for the governor. For example, the Democratic governor of Mississippi in 1979 had what appeared to be a very comfortable majority in both houses of the legislature, since the Democratic margin was 50 to 1 in the Senate and 119 to 3 in the House.

Yet, in practice the governor of Mississippi might find himself in much the same position as the Republican Governor of Nevada, who was faced by a 15 to 5 Democratic majority in the senate and a 25 to 15 Democratic majority in the house. Both governors needed "enough" votes to get their legislation passed. While the governor of Nevada might have had an edge in starting with at least a nucleus of Republican votes, he still had to beg or borrow the additional votes necessary. The governor of Mississippi found himself in much the same situation. He also started with a block of goodwill votes that were the result of his election as governor. However, he, too, had to beg or borrow enough votes to produce that magic "one more than the opposition."

If those solidly Democratic states with legislatures that in the last ten years have consistently ranged from 80 to 100 percent Democratic are added to the states with divided party control, there are approximately thirty-seven states in which the traditional views on party control must be carefully reexamined. In fact, the phenomenon of divided party control between the governor and the legislature has become so widespread in the last thirty years that it is necessary to readjust our concept of this relationship and think less in terms of "party" and more in terms of "votes," any vote. A recent study shows that there has been a steady rise in divided government. For example, from 1930 to 1950, the governor and the majority of the legislature did not belong to the same party only 37.5 percent of the time. However, from 1952 to 1966, the figure rose to 46.8 percent, while from 1970 to 1974 it was 51.8 percent.[2]

Table 5 illustrates this point by presenting in more detail the situation in regard to divided control in the forty-nine states with partisan legislatures as of January 1979. In that year there were nineteen states that had a Democratic governor and a Democratic house and senate and four states with a Republican governor and a Republican house and senate. Thus there were only twenty-three states that fit the pattern of party control upon which most of our traditional thinking about executive-legislative relations is based.

On the other hand, there were twenty-six states (over one-half of the forty-nine states being considered) which did not fit the traditional pattern. In eighteen of these states, the governor found himself faced with both houses of the legislature under the control of the opposition party while in six others the governor's party controlled only one house. The remaining two states presented rather bizarre patterns. Minnesota had a Republican governor, but the lower house was evenly divided and the upper house was controlled by the Democrats. In Washington, on the other hand, the Democrats controlled both the governorship and the senate, but the lower house was evenly divided.

Except for the evenly divided houses, there was nothing particularly unusual about the fact that in 1980 slightly over one-half of all states had a pattern of divided party control. To this group should be added the twelve Democratic states in which the governor had an overwhelming majority of his party in both houses of the Legislature. While these states did not represent divided control, they represented party domination, which was so complete that the governor could not use "party" as a basis for appealing to the legislature to pass his program. Thus in 1980, 75 percent of the states did not fit the traditional party pattern of executive-legislative relations.

TABLE 5
DIVIDED CONTROL: GOVERNOR AND LEGISLATURE IN 1979

Democratic Governor and Democratic House and Senate		Republican Governor and Democratic House and Senate	Democratic Governor and Republican House and Senate
Alabama	Mississippi	Delaware	Arizona
Arkansas	Missouri	Illinois	Colorado
California	New Jersey	Louisiana	Idaho
Connecticut	New Mexico	Michigan	Kansas
Florida	North Carolina	Nevada	North Dakota
Georgia	Oklahoma	Ohio	Utah
Hawaii	Rhode Island	Oregon	Wyoming
Kentucky	South Carolina	Tennessee	
Maryland	West Virginia	Texas	
Massachusetts		Virginia	
		Wisconsin	

Republican Governor and Republican House and Senate	Republican Governor and One House Democratic	Democratic Governor and One House Republican
Indiana	Alaska	Maine
Iowa	Pennsylania	Montana
South Dakota		New Hampshire
Vermont		New York

Republican Governor One House Democratic One House even		Democratic Governor One House Democratic One House even
Minnesota		Washington

SOURCE: *The Book of the States, 1980–81* (Lexington, Ky.: Council of State Governments, 1980), pp. 85, 110.
NOTE: Nebraska was omitted from this table. It has a nonpartisan, unicameral legislature.

Therefore, in three-quarters of the states, the governor had to find methods other than an appeal to party loyalty to build a block of votes sufficient to secure the passage of his legislation. How this feat was accomplished in these rather difficult circumstances is a matter covered in some detail in a succeeding chapter on the governor's role in policy formation.

The Governor's Role in Intergovernmental Relations

While there is no generally accepted definition of the term "intergovernmental relations," it can be reasonably interpreted to mean not only federal-state relations but also federal-local relations, relations among the states, relations between a state and its local units of government, and even inter-local relationships. Thus, the governor as the chief spokesman for the state represents it in its dealings with the federal government, with other states, and with local units, particularly the state's municipalities.

In regard to the first relationship, a good case can be made for the increasing importance of state-federal relations in recent years. For example, in 1977 the average state obtained about 22 percent of its revenue from the federal government. There were some states with higher totals, such as Arkansas with 31 percent, Vermont with 30 percent, Alabama with 28 percent, and Rhode Island and Hawaii with 27 percent. Even some of the most populous states such as Pennsylvania showed a 23 percent dependence upon federal funds. At the other end of the scale were other large states, including New York, California, Ohio, Connecticut, Indiana, and New Jersey, which were in the 18 to 19 percent bracket.[3]

Not only does a significant part of the states' revenue come from the federal government, but this percentage has risen sharply in the last twenty years. Therefore, it seems logical to assume that if power follows dollars, then the impact of the federal government is greater today on the state government than it was twenty years ago. However, this impact may be more apparent than real. For example, taking the latest period for which data is available as our base, we find that over the period from 1966 to 1975 federal grants to the states increased from $11.7 billion to $36.1 billion, which is a sharp increase in actual dollars. However, over this period federal grants constituted a fairly stable share of the states' total revenues, since "they amounted to 25.5% in the fiscal year 1966 and 23.4% in the fiscal year 1975."[4] As was pointed out above, the 1977 percentage (22) was somewhat lower but still falls in the 20 percent range.

The main question, though, remains as to whether or not the amount of money involved is sufficient to change the relationship of the federal government to the states. Taken over a thirty-year period there is no doubt of the federal impact. However, seen in a shorter view, say, the last ten years, the federal impact may have been exaggerated. In the first place, as noted above, federal grants to the states constitute a fairly stable percentage of total state revenues and certainly have not increased significantly over the past ten years. In the second place, in several instances, including revenue sharing, there is a pass-through provision that automatically assigns a portion of the federal funds to local governments within the states.

Thus there is some reason to think that any major changes have occurred because of the way in which the federal government now structures its grants-in-aid, not because of the amount of money involved. The two principal new forms in recent years have been the block grant, of which the Law Enforcement Assistance Act is perhaps one of the best examples, and the revenue-sharing system. The states are given considerably more freedom to operate with these new forms than with categorical grants.

On the other hand, we should not overemphasize these changes. If you add to the pass-through provisions the fact that about 90 percent of federal funds still come to the states under categorical grants such as those for highways and social welfare, there may not have been as substantial a change in recent years in the position of the states vis-à-vis the federal government as the overall dollar totals would suggest.

In spite of recent legislation and several significant Supreme Court decisions, the position of the states in the federal system is relatively unchanged. As will be pointed out subsequently, this does not mean that the states have not had to change their ways of administration. However, it does suggest that most of the recent legislation, particularly revenue sharing, while a significant factor in state financial affairs, has been of much greater significance to the local units of government. This is primarily true because revenue sharing makes up only about 14 percent of the total federal grants to the states and two-thirds of this amount goes to local government.

The Advisory Commission on Intergovernmental Relations (ACIR) estimates that about 26.4 percent of total federal aid to the states passes through to localities. These "pass-through" funds have now become a significant factor in local government finances. Many of these local units have become dependent on federal funds for a major part of their budgets. A substantial number of our major cities, particularly the older cities with an urban core problem, would probably go bankrupt if the federal government suddenly changed its formulas. For example, a recent ACIR study that surveyed federal aid to the fifteen largest cities (excluding New York) for the years 1967, 1976, and 1978 found that for 1978 these cities "are getting from the federal government 47.5 percent as much money as they are raising from their own sources."[5] The estimate for New York is 45.6 percent which is very close to the average for the fifteen cities. These figures contrast sharply with the 5.2 percent these fifteen cities received from Washington in 1967 and the 28.1 percent in 1976. However, the Sun Belt cities, which have larger tax bases probably because they are more diffused geographically, receive less from the federal government than the average city of similar size. For example, Denver, Colorado, received 25.9 percent of its income from the federal government in 1978 as compared to 1.2 percent in 1967. However, this 25.9 percent is only about one-half that of the older cities.

Thus while recent changes in the federal grant-in-aid system at first glance might seem to have altered the position of the states in relation to the federal government, this does not actually appear to be the case. Revenue sharing has been significant, but it is not nearly so significant as the new block grants and these, in turn, are not so significant as the almost 500 categorical grants which are still in place. Furthermore, the "pass-through" provisions of the revenue-sharing act have required that two-thirds of these funds go directly to local governments without state intervention. Thus, the act may have changed the balance between the municipalities and the states more than it has between the states and the federal government.

On the other hand, the whole question of federal funds has become a very significant one on an intrastate basis and has definitely influenced the role of the governor because in each state there has been an open struggle between the governor and the legislature for the control of federal funds. This has been true not only of revenue sharing, but also of block grants, and even of the traditional grants which states have been receiving from the federal government for many years.

In some states federal funds, including the state's part of revenue sharing funds, have been placed in the general fund and the legislature has controlled these in much the same way as state appropriations. In other states where the legislature technically appropriates federal funds, the appropriation has not been a method of actual control. In these states the governor has played an extremely significant role not only in the state's part of the money from revenue sharing but also in the established grants, and perhaps has had his greatest impact on the new block grants such as that from LEAA. In many states the governor has virtually controlled the distribution of these funds and thus has added another weapon to his political arsenal.

The struggle between the governor and the legislature for the control of federal funds generally has developed when these funds became a significant part of the state's revenue. While this has not been a vital issue in many states, it had become important enough in thirteen states by 1976 to require legislation. In these states the legislation usually provides that all federal funds must go into the state's general fund and must be specifically appropriated by the legislature before they can be expended by the executive branch.

The fight became quite heated in Pennsylvania and Colorado. In Pennsylvania, Governor Milton Shapp brought suit against the legislature over the type of legislation described above. He claimed that the general assembly had exceeded its power. His argument was based on the fact that the legislation required that all federal funds go into the state treasury and that these funds could be spent only after appropriation by the legislature. Thus, from the governor's perspective the statute violated the doctrine of the separation of powers. Among other things, the governor contended in his suit that the final control of federal funds must rest with the executive branch at the state level. He argued that "While the General Assembly has the authority to appropriate state funds, only the Governor has the right to allocate the spending of federal monies. Delays in the appropriation process may mean that Pennsylvania loses federal dollars to other jurisdictions."[6] The state legislature contended that it was the primary responsibility of the legislature under the constitution to appropriate not only state funds but all funds. In other words, it was the traditional power of the purse argument. This case was appealed to the Supreme Court of Pennsylvania, which held that the legislature did have the power to appropriate not only state funds but also federal funds within the guidelines set out by the federal government.[7]

In its discussion of the rationale for its decision, the Pennsylvania Supreme Court found that from 1961 to 1965 "the annual appropriation of the General Assembly contained a general provision appropriating grants made to the Commonwealth of various federally funded programs to state agencies involved in the programs of the administration." It also found that " . . . the legislature's control over funds was, in the General Assembly's own terms, 'minimal' . . . " But, the court added that "The Legislature did, of course, maintain exclusive control over appropriations of state matching and general revenue sharing."[8] The court also found that the constitution of Pennsylvania, like many other state constitutions, provides that no funds be expended from the state treasury without an appropriation. This combination of legislative practice and constitutional authority was found by the justices to be a completely persuasive basis for recognizing total legislative power over appropriations. The real question was whether the term "appropriation" covers both state and federal funds. The Pennsylvania Supreme Court felt that the term did cover federal funds, even though the legislature had to accept federal funds within whatever guidelines the federal government specified. Once accepted, the court argued, the legislature could establish priorities within whatever general categories were set out by Congress.

On the other hand, the Colorado Supreme Court several years earlier in 1972 in the case of *MacMannus v. Love* had taken a different view.[9] This case was narrower in scope than the Pennsylvania case since it revolved around the question of the Colorado legislature appropriating future federal funds. However, in *MacMannus v. Love,* the Colorado Supreme Court found that while the general assembly had authority to appropriate state funds to match federal grants, it did *not* have the authority to appropriate federal funds which had not yet come into the state treasury. The exact wording of the section of the Colorado act in question reads as follows: "Any federal or cash funds received by an agency in excess of the appropriation shall not be expended without additional legislative appropriation." The trial court in which the case originated held that the general assembly had the authority to appropriate such federal funds.

However, the Colorado Supreme Court held on appeal that the legislative limitation, quoted above, was in violation of the constitutional doctrine of separation of powers and, consequently, it reversed the lower court. Again, there was no disagreement on the power of the legislature to appropriate state funds or even about its appropriating currently held federal funds. The question in the case was whether or not the legislative body could require that federal funds which had not yet come into the treasury be spent only after an appropriation by the general assembly. The Colorado Supreme Court held that what the legislature tried to do by this act was to "attempt to limit the executive branch in the administration of federal funds to be received by it directly from agencies of the federal government and unconnected with any state appropriation. In fact such funds, to be received in the future, may often be unanticipated or even unknown at the time of the passage of the bill."[10] Therefore, the Colorado Supreme Court argued that the appropriation power of the general assembly relates only to state funds and that federal contributions are not subject to appropriation by the legislature.

Thus two state supreme courts in fairly recent cases have arrived at different findings on the question of the power of the legislature to appropriate federal funds. It is doubtful that the end of this argument has been heard. Although I am a strong supporter of state government, it seems quite likely that the lone dissenter in the Pennsylvania case may be correct in the long run. His dissent was based on the supremacy clause of the federal constitution. He argued that when Congress appropriates for a specific purpose, the state legislature must follow congressional dictates if they accept the funds in spite of the state legislature's right to appropriate under the state constitution. Thus when a case of this nature is appealed to the United States Supreme Court, that Court may well rely on the supremacy clause to curtail the power of the state legislature to "reappropriate" federal funds. On the other hand, they may go along with the Pennsylvania rather than the Colorado interpretation. However, such a ruling would certainly present some real difficulties for Congress in its attempt to promote a particular national purpose through the requirements attached to federal grants-in-aid.

The whole issue could become slightly less significant if Congress moves in the direction of a larger program of revenue sharing and greater flexibility through increasing block grants. At the time this was written, the reverse appeared to be true since Congress was seriously considering a cut rather than an increase in revenue sharing. An increase in the number of block grants also seems a possibility. In any event, grants in some form undoubtedly will continue, and the struggle over their control at the state level is unlikely to be settled until we have a definite United States Supreme Court decision on the question.

It is not the thesis of this section that federal grants are insignificant. On the contrary, they are quite significant and have become an important part of the states' income. If this were not so, there would be no governor suing the legislature as was the case in Colorado over the question of control of federal funds. If the control of federal funds were insignificant, it is unlikely that the executive and legislative branches of state government would be engaged in lawsuits on the question. On the other hand, the pass-through provisions of revenue sharing and the formulas used in determining block grants in a great many categories may actually be more significant to the relationship of the states to their municipalities than to the relationship of the states to the federal government.

Of course, it should be pointed out that any drastic change in the finances of its municipalities eventually affects the state, which the governor and legislature of New York have already discovered. Consequently, any major federal changes in revenue sharing that will reduce the municipalities' income probably would have to be reflected in changed priorities in the state budget in order to take up some of the slack from the loss of federal funds. At present the governor in most states has no role in the approval of those revenue sharing funds going directly to the municipalities. Nevertheless, he may find that he will have to deal with changes in state-local relations that have been caused by shifts in federal policy.

The Governor's Formal Powers

The legal and institutional framework in which the governor operates is made up primarily of those provisions of the state statutes and constitution that affect the way in which the governor operates. These provisions are difficult to describe in a short, meaningful phrase and are frequently lumped together in studies of the governor under the general rubric of "the governor's formal powers." Since this phrase is a convenient one, it is often used in this study. It is a generally accurate expression if two reservations are kept in mind. The first of these is that the constitutional and statutory provisions that govern the office may provide for either powers or limitations on those powers. In short, while the constitution giveth, the constitution also taketh away. For example, the provisions which give the governor the authority to appoint department heads are generally regarded as a "power," and the lack of such authority is generally seen as a weakness. Therefore, when forced to rank this power in some way, we generally use the not too scholarly device of counting the number of appointees whom the statutes authorize the governor to appoint. This problem is discussed later in this section under the heading "The Appointing Power." However, the point to remember about the first caveat is that while the constitution and statutes of the state may give the governor certain powers of appointment, they can also reduce that power. This reduction is evidenced not only by a failure to grant the appointing power to the governor but by provisions for the selection of department heads in some other manner, such as by popular election, by the legislature, or by a board.

The second reservation to be noted is that there are certain other formal powers which are not, strictly speaking, "powers" at all. Rather, they are provisions of the constitution and statutes which can either increase or decrease gubernatorial power. The length of the governor's term (two or four years) and the provisions governing whether or not he can succeed himself are generally set out by the constitution of each state. However, the length of a governor's term is not, in itself, a "power," even though a long term with succession probably can be translated into power. It is widely assumed that a four-year term rather than a two-year term strengthens the hand of the governor in dealing with the legislature because it gives the governor not only time to plan a program but also generally from two to four sessions to try to secure enactment. It is also assumed that if the governor can immediately succeed himself, he is in a stronger position than if he cannot. Thus, the goal of those who believe in a strong governor would be for the governor of all states to have a four-year term with unlimited succession. This goal is based on the assumption that four-year terms with unlimited succession will, in fact, strengthen the hand of the governor in policy formation.

This assumption received considerable support among those interviewed, including governors, members of the governors' staffs, legislators, and department heads. Almost all of these "usually well informed sources" felt that long tenure and strong powers of appointment were in practice, as well as in theory, a considerable help to the governor. Furthermore, there have been several studies which give considerable credence to the idea that the formal powers of the governor can be translated into actual or operational power. This seems to be true especially in his dealings with the legislature and, to a more limited extent, in his dealings with administrators in the executive branch.

One of the most recent studies to touch directly on this problem is E. Lee Bernick's analysis of the perceived importance of the governor's formal powers as compared to his informal powers in dealing with the legislature.[11] His findings were based on a questionnaire survey of senators in eleven states. In his questionnaire he asked the senators to list in the order of importance the "tools" or "powers" which they perceive to be the most significant for the governor in dealing with the legislature. His hypothesis was that the governor's informal powers would be ranked as more important than his formal powers. His findings, however, did not support this

hypothesis since he found that the senators ranked budget formation (a formal power) as the most important of the governor's powers. The second ranked power was an informal one, the ability of
the governor to muster popular support. However, ranking third
and fourth were the formal powers of control over agencies and the
veto.

Bernick further refined his analysis to control for weak and
strong gubernatorial states by correlating the fourteen powers
which were mentioned by the senators with weak governor and
strong governor states as indicated by the formal powers on Schlesinger's index. In his preliminary analysis he found that the rank
order correlation for the fourteen items mentioned by the senators
was almost a perfect .915. However, when he considered only the
five highest ranked items, a distinct difference appeared in the
choices of the senators in the weak governor states as compared to
those in the strong governor states. For example, senators from the
states where the governor had weak formal powers ranked popular
support as the number one gubernatorial power. This is a distinct
contrast to the views of the senators from the strong governor
states who ranked budget formation as the most important of the
governor's powers and ranked popular support in only fourth
place. Bernick concludes that "in short, governors who possess a
significant amount of formal powers are most apt to be perceived
as relying upon them as major means of achieving legislative success. On the other hand, weak governors (with regard to formal
powers) are viewed as depending upon informal powers at their disposal."[12]

Bernick's study tends to reinforce the conclusions reached by Ira
Sharkansky some ten years earlier when he found that the governor
played a crucial role in the budgetary process.[13] Sharkansky also
found that the governor was more influential in the budgetary process in those states in which he could succeed himself and where
there were relatively few elected officials to compete with him for
influence in budgetary politics.

The sections of this chapter that follow are based on the assumption that the governor's formal "powers" do make a difference in
his ability to set public policy. As noted above, this seems to be true
in cases where the governor exercises a strong budgeting power. As

two of the following sections demonstrate, it also seems to be true in cases in which the governor has a strong tenure potential or can exercise considerable appointing power.

Tenure Potential

The tenure potential of the governor actually has two major aspects. The first of these is the length of the governor's term and the second is the number of terms a governor can succeed himself. Viewed from both these aspects, the tenure potential of the governor has increased markedly over the last thirty years. For example, as late as 1952 only twenty-eight states had a four-year term, and only fifteen states of this group permitted the governor to succeed himself. The remaining twenty states still had a two-year term although all of them allowed the governor to succeed himself for at least one term. Thus, in the two-year states he had the possibility, but certainly not the guarantee, of at least four years of service if he could be reelected.

The changes in tenure potential by the late 1970s are very substantial. An examination of Table 6 shows that forty-six states had a four-year term by 1980. Consequently, the governor in 90 percent of the states now has at least a full four years in which to establish his policies. In addition, his chance for a second four-year term also has greatly increased. In twenty-three states (versus fifteen in 1952) he can succeed himself for one additional term. In another eighteen states he can stay in office as long as he is able to secure his reelection. Only Kentucky, Mississippi, New Mexico, South Carolina, and Virginia of the four-year states now probibit the governor from succeeding himself. As a result of these changes, the governor's tenure potential, at least in legal terms, has never been higher. If he has the political skills to capitalize on his expanded tenure potential, the increased time in office should enhance the governor's role in policy formation.

Another development which may strengthen the governorship is the "team" election of the governor and lieutenant governor. In 1952 there were no states which had this arrangement. However, by 1980 almost one-half (twenty-one) of the four-year states had the governor-lieutenant governor "ticket system," although none of the states which were still holding to a two-year term had adopted

TABLE 6
THE GOVERNOR'S TENURE POTENTIAL

States with a Four-Year Term, Immediate Succession, and No Restrictions on Reelection			
Arizona	Illinois	Montana	Washington
California	Iowa	New York	Wisconsin
Colorado	Massachusetts	North Dakota	Wyoming
Connecticut	Michigan	Texas	
Idaho	Minnesota	Utah	
States with a Four-Year Term, Immediate Succession, but Governor is Limited to Two Successive Terms			
Alabama	Indiana	Nebraska	Oregon
Alaska	Kansas	Nevada	Pennsylvania
Delaware[a]	Louisiana	New Jersey	South Dakota
Florida	Maine	North Carolina[a]	Tennessee[b]
Georgia	Maryland	Ohio	West Virginia
Hawaii[a]	Missouri[a]	Oklahoma	
States with a Four-Year Term, Governor Restricted to One Term Only			
Kentucky	New Mexico	Virginia	
Mississippi	South Carolina		
States with a Two-Year Term, Immediate Succession			
Arkansas	Rhode Island		
New Hampshire	Vermont		

SOURCE: *The Book of the States, 1980–81* (Lexington, Ky.: Council of State Governments, 1980), p. 170.

[a]Absolute two term limitation, but terms not necessarily consecutive.

[b]After two consecutive terms, the governor must wait four years to be eligible to run for a third term.

this plan. While experience with this arrangement is limited, there is some reason to argue that the plan may be one which will strengthen the governor's role in policy formation. Its most obvious consequence is that it gives the governor a member of his own party in the lieutenant governor's chair. Those advocating the plan assume that since the lieutenant governor is elected on the same platform as the governor, he will be at least sympathetic to the governor's principal objectives. Thus, the lieutenant governor is less likely to try to block the governor's policy initiative and may even be of some help to him. The greatest potential for rendering such help, or, by the same token, for hindering the governor, is found in those states where the lieutenant governor presides over the upper house of the legislature. The presiding officer of most legislative bodies has a considerable influence on the passage of legislation, particularly through his power to refer bills to friendly or unfriendly committees and through parliamentary rulings which may expedite or block the passage of legislation. Thus, a cooperative presiding officer in the form of a lieutenant governor of the same party is in a position to help the governor and the leader of the majority party (if the party is a real factor) get the governor's bills passed. Whether this system actually works as well in practice as its proponents claim is still a matter of conjecture because of the human factors involved. Many lieutenant governors run for the second spot on the ticket with a view toward moving up to the number one spot.[14] Such aspirations might, at best, dictate a little subtle foot dragging in the upper house so that the governor will not look too good to the voters. At worst, a lieutenant governor who has his mind set on being a candidate for the governorship in the next election can be a positive menace to the governor's program in the senate.

It does not take a confirmed cynic, but only an observer of the state political scene, to have some doubts about the efficacy of the "ticket system" even in those states where political parties carry enough weight to make a difference. In the solidly Democratic states and in most of the normally Democratic and normally Republican states, the lieutenant governor is more likely to be the governor's adversary rather than his chief aide. This, of course, is particularly true in the absence of a "ticket system," where the governor and lieutenant governor are elected separately. A good example of what can happen under this arrangement was the feud which developed during Governor Edmund (Jerry) Brown's second term in California between Brown, a Democrat, and Mike Curb, a Republican who was elected lieutenant governor. Since the California constitution specifies that the governor's powers may be exercised by the lieutenant governor during the chief executive's absence from the state and since the governor was a presidential candidate, the stage was set for a confrontation.

During 1979 Lieutenant Governor Curb took advantage of Brown's absence to appoint a superior court judge and to sign an order relaxing California's air pollution standards. Neither action was approved by Brown. The situation had deteriorated to such a point in late 1979 that Governor Brown requested the California Supreme Court to rule that he retained his powers when away from California. He argued that since he traveled by plane he could stay in touch by phone and hence was "not effectively absent" from the state.[15] The court, however, refused to restrict the actions of the lieutenant governor when Brown was out of the state. Nevertheless, it did hold that when Brown returned, he could revoke the lieutenant governor's appointments if those appointments had not yet been confirmed by the senate.

However, even in those states in which the lieutenant governor is of the same party as the governor, he or she still may have aspirations for the governorship. For example, Mary Anne Krupsak, the lieutenant governor of New York who was elected with Governor Hugh Carey in 1975, ran against him in 1979 for the Democratic nomination. Experience thus far with gubernatorial politics indicates that most lieutenant governors have aspirations for the governorship. Further, the statistics on gubernatorial elections show that the lieutenant governor has a very good chance at the top spot. As long as this remains the case, it seems reasonable to expect more competition than cooperation between governor and lieutenant governor.

The Appointing Power

The appointing power of the governor is a useful tool for him in at least two ways. In the first place, the governor's control over the executive branch is strengthened if he can appoint the heads of the major departments of state government. The presence of an individual appointed by the governor at the top of the administrative heirarchy in an agency provides the governor with a channel of communication to that agency. Consequently, the governor's wishes are more likely to be carried out in the administration of agency programs than would be the case if the agency were headed by an official not selected by the governor. For many reasons, including an unresponsive bureaucracy in most states, the governor's control even in an agency headed by a gubernatorial appointee is not as strong as it might appear on the surface. However, in the relative world of state politics he has a better chance of exercising greater control over the policies of these agencies than over those that are not headed by his appointees. In the second place, the governor's appointing power when used as patronage can be a useful tool in building support in the legislature and thus help the governor in achieving a legislative bloc necessary for the passage of his administration bills. With the recent growth of the division in party control between the governor and the legislature this power may be reassuming some of the importance it had in the earlier days of widespread patronage when few states had merit systems for the selection of employees.

Table 7 shows the percentage of state officials appointed by the governor in each state. The potential positions covered are secretary of state, attorney general, treasurer, adjutant general, administration, agriculture, banking, budget, civil rights, commerce, community affairs, consumer affairs, corrections, data processing, disaster preparedness, education (chief state school officer), higher education, elections administration, employment services, energy resources, finance, general services, health, highway patrol, highways, historic preservation, industrial development, insurance, labor and industrial relations, licensing, mental health, natural resources, parks and recreation, personnel, planning, post-audit, pre-audit, public library, public utility regulation, purchasing, social services, solid waste, taxation, tourism, transportation and welfare. If an individual performs more than one of the functions listed above, he is counted only once.

As seen in Table 7, New York is the highest ranking state since the governor appoints 89 percent of the administrative officials, followed by Virginia with 86 percent and Hawaii with 82 percent. At the lower end of the scale are found South Carolina, where the governor appoints only 21 percent of the administrative officials, Texas and Georgia with rankings of 24 percent and 27 percent, respectively. At about midpoint of the range are found Utah, West Virginia, and Colorado with 49 percent and Maryland and Tennessee with 48 percent. These states fall closest to the median of the series which is 48.5 percent.

TABLE 7
THE PERCENTAGE OF SELECTED STATE ADMINISTRATIVE
OFFICIALS APPOINTED BY THE GOVERNOR IN EACH STATE, 1980

State	Percentage	State	Percentage
New York	89	Colorado	49
		Maryland	48
Virginia	86	Tennessee	48
Hawaii	82	Idaho	47
		Wisconsin	47
Illinois	76	Wyoming	46
California	76	Montana	44
Iowa	71	Arizona	42
		Arkansas	42
Minnesota	67	Mississippi	42
Pennsylvania	67	Kansas	41
Louisiana	64	Kentucky	40
New Hampshire	63	Alabama	40
Indiana	63	Washington	40
New Jersey	56	Oklahoma	38
Vermont	56	Maine	38
Massachusetts	55	Nevada	38
Nebraska	54	Michigan	36
New Mexico	54	Florida	36
Ohio	54	North Dakota	34
Connecticut	51	Alaska	33
Delaware	50		
North Carolina	50	Oregon	29
Rhode Island	50	Missouri	29
South Dakota	50	Georgia	27
		Texas	24
Utah	49	South Carolina	21
West Virginia	49		

NOTE: This analysis is based on the table, "State Administrative Officials, Methods of Selection," in *The Book of the States, 1980–81* (Lexington, Ky.: Council of State Governments, 1980), pp. 195–97.

A careful observer will have noted that there are forty-six positions listed above. However, not all forty-six of these positions are
actually found in any one state. The greatest number, forty-four, is
found in Massachusetts, and the smallest number, seventeen, in
Hawaii. Consequently, in order to compare one state with another,
a ratio of officials to gubernatorial appointees was developed and
expressed in percentage terms. For example, in New York there are
thirty-seven of the possible forty-six officials listed. In that state the
governor appoints thirty-three out of these thirty-seven officials.
Thus, he achieves an appointment ratio of 89 percent, which happens to be the highest ratio for all the states. This same calculation
was made for each state and the results are shown in Table 7.

Another way to evaluate the appointing power is to place the
states in rough groupings according to the governor's scope of appointment. If this is done, the picture which emerges is that of a
rather weak governorship. In only twenty-two states does the governor appoint 50 percent or more of the state's administrative officials. In the remainder of the states his appointments range downward from 49 percent to only 21 percent.

Either of these methods will give some idea of the scope of the
governor's appointing power. However, it should be realized that
this method of comparison reveals nothing of the actual appointing
power of the governor within a given state. For example, it is essential to know not only the number of the governor's appointees but
also the importance of the positions they hold. To take an extreme
example, if the governor of a state appoints only the secretary of
state, the treasurer, and the auditor, he will be credited with three
appointments. However, these three appointments are not nearly
equal in importance to those in another state where the governor
appoints the director of finance, the budget director, and the commissioner of highways. Like anything else that is tabulated, the results depend upon what is counted and here are simply counted the
number of administrative positions listed above. Such a tabulation
gives us a rough idea of the governor's appointing power in terms
of numbers, and, judged by that criterion, it shows rather clearly
that in New York the governor's appointing power is considerably
stronger than in South Carolina. On the other hand, it does not dis-
close whether the 21 percent of the positions the governor appoints

in South Carolina are important or not. The data on which to base such a judgment are not readily available although the names of the officials whom the governor does or does not appoint are available in *The Book of the States*. This source reports which officials in New York and in South Carolina are appointed by the governor, which are elected, and which are selected in other ways, for example, by boards. However, the problem of judging the importance of these officials remains. Therefore, the survey above, while it is useful, is certainly not definitive in speaking to the question of the governor's actual power of appointment either comparatively or within the state.

It is generally felt that a broad appointing power is an advantage to a governor in his dealing with the various department heads and even with the legislature. This point has been substantiated to a limited extent by some of the quantitative studies, particularly those of Ira Sharkansky.[16] However, there is no definitive empirical basis for the traditional assumption that the governor's appointing power really helps him in getting his measures through the legislature or in the establishment of public policy.

Based on my interviews, I have concluded that a broad appointing power is, indeed, useful to the governor, but I cannot prove it quantitatively. Nor do the data presented above reveal anything very significant in terms of the governor's actual power either on an interstate basis or an intrastate basis. One of the problems with any formulation of the governor's formal powers that includes the appointing power as an element is that the formula generally gives equal weight to each position the governor appoints. Such equality is not in accordance with the real importance of the different positions. For example, I think that most governors and legislators would agree that it is more important for the governor to appoint the budget director than the secretary of state. However, about the only supporting evidence we have of any significance is Sharkansky's article on the impact of the governor versus his department heads on the budget. In this study he shows rather clearly that in those states where the governor has a broad appointing power, he does better policywise through the budget than in those states in which there are a number of elected officials who may compete with him.

The question is not so much one of patronage but simply that the governor needs people in key positions who think in the same terms as he does. For example, there have been several midwestern governors who were elected as Democrats but whose fiscal conservatism has made it possible for any of them to work with a director of finance who espoused a brand of fiscal conservatism that might be difficult to distinguish from that generally associated with traditional Republicanism. However, a "new model" Republican governor who believes in the state government taking an active role in mental health might get along with a rather thinly disguised Democrat in the position of mental health commissioner since they might agree on the necessity for additional governmental spending in this area.

It is probably more important for the governor to have department heads who agree with him on his basic fundamental approach to government rather than to have department heads who are members of his own party. However, except for a few departments in which expertise is considered a key factor, such as mental health or public health, it is unusual to find a governor going outside his party if he can possibly avoid doing so.

In spite of the fact that the data given above are purely quantitative, they do give us a rough idea of the governor's appointing power at least in terms of its scope. It does not, however, tell us very much about the significance of these appointments in terms of the governor's supervision of the executive branch. In this aspect of the governor's functions, it is important for the governor to control the appointments of key members of the executive branch. The stress on the word "key" is deliberate since it makes very little difference who appoints the secretary of state, but it makes a great deal of difference who appoints the director of finance, the budget officer, and perhaps the chief revenue officer. In any state with a self-respecting political machine it is also useful for the governor to appoint the person in charge of highways and other public works.

Depending upon the governor's policies and perhaps even his platform, it may be crucial to him to control through his appointments the educational system, the programs for the handicapped, or other functions in which he has a particular interest.

The federal government has become so embedded in some departments, for example, in welfare and employment security (i.e., the operation of the state employment service) that the governor has little control over these departments. While he may appoint the department head, the heads of the major divisions, such as the director of the state employment office, are quite likely to be under the merit system. Furthermore, the major financing (90 percent) of this division comes from federal funds. Hence, the governor is in too weak a position to control these divisions.

Because of the complexities in the appointing process only touched on above, the picture of the governor's appointing power is only a broad-brush treatment of the governor's control over the executive branch. It has been suggested that this control improves his ability to get his program through the legislative branch. However, a simple tabulation of his appointments does not prove anything in terms of the gubernatorial appointing power except to give some idea of the relative scope of these appointments. Moreover, the results of even a simple tabulation depends on what you count. While the forty-six functions selected by *The Book of the States* seem reasonable, they certainly are not equal in value and could not, by any stretch of the imagination, be weighted the same. Neither does it seem important that one of the states does not have one of these forty-six listed functions. As a matter of fact, most of the states get along very well with considerably fewer than the forty-six listed.

The fact that the governor appoints an official does not necessarily mean that the position is one of great significance, nor does the governor's failure to appoint mean that the position is of lesser importance. For example, forty-eight of the fifty adjutant generals are picked by the governors while only nine of the fifty heads of the departments of education are selected by the governors. The absence of gubernatorial appointments in the education field does not signify that education is an unimportant state function. Rather, it seems to reflect education's long-term, alleged disassociation from "politics."

The concept of gubernatorial appointment, its importance, and its relation to the legislature is an interesting one. However, it is difficult to get at the reasons for the variety of patterns found unless the person making the study knows the state intimately. For example, it would take a person who knew the political history of the states very well to explain why eight states—Alabama, Indiana, Kentucky, Massachusetts, Nevada, North Carolina, New Hampshire, and Tennessee—do not require that *any* of their gubernatorial appointees be confirmed by the senate. It would also be necessary to explain why there are five states (Hawaii, Kansas, Missouri, New Jersey, and Virginia) which require that *all* gubernatorial appointments be confirmed.

This is an interesting problem because it would be generally supposed that the governor would be stronger in those states which do not require senatorial confirmation of his appointments. Therefore, the question arises of whether the statistical or the observational method should be used. Under the former, Virginia would be considered a strong gubernatorial appointment state because 86 percent of its administrative officials are appointed by the governor. Under the latter we might see it as a weak gubernatorial appointment state because Virginia requires that *all* of these appointees be approved by the legislature. Alabama, on the other hand, rates only a 40 percent grade on gubernatorial appointments, but the governor of Alabama appoints all 40 percent of his selectees without confirmation by either house of the legislature. The evaluation of the strength and weakness of a governor's appointing power is a difficult task and one that is hard to prove statistically. As the late V. O. Key used to say, perhaps what our statistical analyses do is pinpoint areas in which we need to do further in-depth studies.

In connection with the governor's appointing power it should also be pointed out that in 1964 Congress passed the Civil Rights Act. While the act itself does not directly affect the governor's appointing power, the accompanying rules and regulations involve the whole gamut of equal opportunity and affirmative action. These regulations, to say nothing of the various court decisions involved, have had the most substantial impact on personnel management practices in the states of any single change since the adoption of the merit principle in most states. The governor usually is not involved personally in a major way in the enforcement of equal opportunity and affirmative action plans. However, the spirit of the act certainly has had an impact on gubernatorial appointments. For example, the governors' staffs in the 1970s were better balanced than in previous years in terms of both women and minorities. It is also true that since the late 1960s, major appointments by most governors have included women, blacks, and chicanos. This is true even in the South, which has long been regarded as being backward in matters of racial and sexual equality. For example, Governor Fob James of Alabama, who was elected in 1978, appointed a black to head the Department of Pensions and Security. This agency is one of the four principal departments of the state government not only in terms of the number of employees and the size of its budget but also in terms of its impact on the citizenry. He also appointed women to several important positions as did Governor George C. Wallace, who preceded James as governor of Alabama. The same situation prevailed in Georgia at least as early as the Carter administration. Former Governor Jimmy Carter, writing in 1975, stated that he had appointed " . . . dozens of qualified black citizens to major policy board positions, so they could participate fully in official deliberations such as those concerning the university system, the corrections system, state law enforcement, all aspects of human resources, the pardon and parole system, and the professional examination boards . . . and many more."[17]

In addition, several states have had a tradition for at least two decades of electing women to major posts. For example, in Alabama over the past twenty years the offices of state treasurer, state auditor, and secretary of state have been filled exclusively by women until the 1978 election in which a man was elected as secretary of state. In addition to these more or less traditional posts, in the last ten years there has been a movement of women into a broader range of major posts within the state. These positions include the election for the second time of a woman as one of the three members of the Alabama Public Service Commission, a body which regulates utilities within the state. In addition, there was the unprecedented election of a woman justice as one of the seven members of the Alabama Supreme Court although one had previously served on the Alabama Court of Appeals.

Under the equal opportunity and affirmative action regulations a governor does not have to advertise a political "vacancy." For example, he would not have to state that he is seeking a department head and consequently would not be required to invite women and minorities to apply. However, as a practical matter he must set an example within his state. Furthermore, as a good political strategist, the governor is not unmindful of the growing political power of minorities and women. Consequently, he has ample political as well as ethical reasons to assume a leadership role in the appointment of women and minorities to important posts in his administration. While discrimination certainly has not been eliminated, those persons appointed on a political basis now tend to reflect more nearly the racial composition of the state and to present a better male-female balance in positions of importance.

In a field like race and minority relations, the governor leads primarily by example and the pattern he sets in his major appointments is an important part of that example. Because women, blacks, and Mexican-Americans are being appointed as department heads, they now can reasonably expect to be a significant factor in state politics or administration. The governor's example also affects many appointments that are made by the heads of agencies in the executive branch. If the governor shows he really means business on equal opportunity and affirmative action, then this cue is usually taken quickly by the departments of the state government. If it is not picked up, the governor has as many ways of reinforcing an affirmative action policy as he has of pushing any other policy. For example, he may reinforce his "cue" through budget cuts or through his refusal to give agencies new or expanded programs unless they agree to staff these programs, at least proportionately, with minorities and women.

While it is difficult to determine how widespread real equal opportunity and affirmative action have become in political posts at the state level, the contrast between going into a governor's office in 1956 and 1976 was striking. Nowhere in 1956 did I find that the governor's principal staff assistant was a woman. In only one state was one of the governor's principal assistants black. However, in 1976 it was not uncommon to find that not only were the receptionists and other clerical staff either blacks or chicanos but also that the governor's principal assistant, press secretary, or principal legislative liaison officer were women. The fact that women and minorities now occupy a number of key positions on the governor's staff was something which I did not expect to find when interviewing. It appears that these changes are more than mere tokenism. While no governor would admit that he is working on a quota basis, the fact that a substantial number of his principal appointees represent minorities or women is a distinct contrast to the gubernatorial staffing pattern of twenty years ago.

Of course, it is also noteworthy that there have been two women in recent years elected governor in their own right. They were Ella Grasso of Connecticut, who was elected to her second four-year term in 1978, and Dixy Lee Ray, who was elected in 1976 to a four-year term in Washington. In addition, there are a number of women who have been elected lieutenant governor. Examples in recent elections are Rose Mofford (Arizona, 1978), Nancy Dick (Colorado, 1978), Jean Sadako King (Hawaii, 1978), Norma Paulus (Oregon, 1977), Nancy Stevenson (South Carolina, 1978), Madeleine Kunin (Vermont, 1978), Thyra Thompson (Wyoming, 1978), and Martha Layne Collins (Kentucky, 1979). It should be noted that Rose Mofford in Arizona, Norma Paulus in Oregon, and Thyra Thompson in Wyoming actually were elected as secretary of state in those jurisdictions. However, the secretary of state in each of the states is first in line of succession to the governorship. Since these states have no lieutenant governors, the person holding office as secretary of state is normally listed as the lieutenant governor.

All of the women who were elected as lieutenant governors in the early 1970s tried to move into the governorship at the next election but none were successful. Mary Anne Krupsak, who was elected lieutenant governor of New York in 1974, ran unsuccessfully in the Democratic primary in 1978 against incumbent Governor Hugh Carey. Thelma Stovall was regarded as a strong possibility for the Democratic nomination in Kentucky in 1979 but she came in last in the primary. Evelyn Gandy sought the Democratic nomination in Mississippi in 1979 but was defeated in the primary. However, she forced her leading opponent into a runoff.

It is also noteworthy that, as of 1977, there were 101 women state senators and 601 women serving as members of the lower house in the various state legislatures. The number of women legislators is more than double that of ten years ago, although women legislators have not yet been elected in sufficient numbers to challenge the traditional male dominance of state legislative bodies. Among women legislators in 1977 there were 7 black women who served as state senators while 39 black women served as members of the lower houses of their respective legislatures. Women legislators, on the whole, tend to be widely scattered in the fifty state legislatures. However, in some seventeen states they constitute at least ten percent of the legislature. If these women legislators were properly organized, they could become a group with some clout in the legislatures of these states.[18]

The Salary/Performance Ratio

One of the criticisms frequently made of state government is that in most states the salary paid state officials is too low in relation to the duties they are expected to perform. This is generally true of the governor who in many states is not a well-paid individual if judged by the present standards of compensation for industrial executives.

The pay scale for the chief executives in the states in 1979 varied from a low of $27,500 in North Dakota to a high of $85,000 in New York with the median salary being $50,000 a year. Only North Dakota pays the governor less than $30,000, but seven states fall in the $30,000 to $40,000 category, and twelve states fall in the $40,000 to $50,000 group. In addition, there were eighteen states in the $50,000 to $60,000 bracket and ten states in the $60,000 to $70,000 range. The high states in terms of the governor's salary are Texas, which pays its governor $71,400, and New York with the top salary of $85,000 a year.

The most popular salary for the governor is an even $50,000 a year since eight states have agreed on that sum as the appropriate gubernatorial salary. A quick glance at these states does not reveal any significant similarities among them in terms of such factors as geographic location, size, or per capita income. For example, although three of these states are in the Southeast, the others are widely scattered with one in the Southwest, one in the Rocky Mountains, one in the Far West, one in the Great Lakes area, and Hawaii in the Pacific. The per capita income in the states in 1978 ranged from a high of $9,439 in Nevada to a low of $6,291 in Alabama, and they varied in size from Arizona, which is number six in area in the nation, to Hawaii, which is forty-seventh in size. The governor's salary seems to be more dependent on the state's political culture than on such concrete factors as per capita income, area, or geographic location. A good example is California, which is first in population, third in area, and third in per capita income, but is thirty-first in salary. The governor of California is paid less than the governors of thirty other states, and his salary is less than one-half of that paid to the governor of New York.

While the $50,000 median salary paid the governor in 1979 may seem very substantial to many readers, it must be considered within the context of the sharp increase in the cost of living in recent years, which affects governors just as it does the average citizen. For example, if the governors' salaries in 1979 are compared to the salaries they received in 1971, we find that their salaries increased 50 percent over the eight-year period, which is not unreasonable when it is compared to the 79 percent increase in the consumer price index for the same period.

It is very difficult to show that there is a direct correlation between the salary paid the governor and the kind of talent that the office will command. Furthermore, there is no hard data to prove that a governor will perform more satisfactorily or even more honestly if his salary is set at a reasonable level. However, the relatively insecure financial position of some governors leaves open the possibility that a governor may use extralegal methods to augment his salary. Thus, the way is opened for expense accounts from large corporations, the selling of pardons, and other devices which may seriously impair the efficiency of administration. Whether the governor actually does use such methods seems to depend largely on the character of the incumbent, and such actions cannot be attributed directly to the low salary paid. It may be, as some writers maintain, that raising the governor's salary would partially remove this temptation and would tend to produce a more honest administration.

The salary paid many of the governors does not compare favorably with that of an executive of even a corporation of medium size. Consequently, some who would be qualified by experience or training for the position will prefer to devote their managerial talent to more lucrative pursuits. Because individuals do not run for the governorship primarily for the monetary rewards of the office, it does not seem entirely logical to assume that raising the salary will have any startling effect on the caliber of the person occupying the office. Those who argue that it will ordinarily use the same line of reasoning as do those who argue for an increase in the salaries of state civil servants. This argument states that the best talent can be obtained only by setting the rate of pay of government employees at a level more nearly comparable to that found in private industry. While this argument may be valid in its application to the civil service, it is not necessarily valid when applied to an elective office, particularly the governorship.

The motives which influence a candidate for the governorship are complex, but on the whole the rewards which he expects from the office tend to be of a personal rather than an economic nature. Social prominence, the opportunity to wield considerable power, and the concept of the governorship as a stepping-stone to becoming a judge, United States senator, or perhaps even a presidential candidate all seem to weigh heavily in this determination. It is probable, therefore, that we cannot expect an increase in the caliber of the candidates for the governorship proportionate to an increase in the salary offered. On the other hand, it seems in keeping with our democratic philosophy of government and a common sense precaution to establish a salary for the governor which will at least enable him to live on his official income without resort to extralegal means. While it must be admitted that few of the state's citizens will have the political availability that is so necessary for a successful candidate, a low salary should not be established as an additional handicap to the well-intentioned citizen seeking the office. Perhaps what is needed is a dual approach, which includes a salary increase in those states where the governor is indeed underpaid and an examination of the possibilities of reducing the cost of campaigning for the office. The latter, perhaps even more than the low salary, is the real barrier for "poor but honest" aspirants to the governorship.

Notes

1. Sarah McCally Morehouse, "The State Political Party and the Policy-Making Process," *American Political Science Review* 67 (March 1973): 60.

2. William J. Keefe and Morris S. Ogul, *The American Legislative Process: Congress and the States,* 4th ed. (Englewood Cliffs, N.J.: Prentice-Hall, 1977), p. 110.

3. David B. Walker and Albert J. Richter, "States and the Impact of Federal Grants," *State Government* 50 (Spring 1977): 83.

4. Ibid.

5. William Steif, "Big Cities Dependency on U.S. Growing," *Birmingham* (Ala.) *Post Herald,* 27 March 1978, sec. A, p. 6.

6. Shapp v. Sloan and the General Assembly of Pennsylvania, Pa., 391 A.2d 595.

7. Ibid.

8. Ibid.

9. MacMannus v. Love, Colo., 499 P.2d 609.

10. Ibid.

11. E. Lee Bernick, "Gubernatorial Tools: Formal vs. Informal," *Journal of Politics* 41 (May 1979): 656-64.

12. Ibid., p. 663.

13. Ira Sharkansky, "Agency Requests, Gubernatorial Support and Budget Success in State Legislatures," *American Political Science Review* 62 (December 1968): 1220-31.

14. Larry Sabato, *Goodbye to Good-Time Charlie: The American Governor Transformed, 1950-1975* (Lexington, Mass.: D.C. Heath, 1978), p. 39.

15. *U.S. News and World Report,* 5 November 1979, p. 53.

16. Sharkansky, "Agency Requests," pp. 1220-31.

17. Jimmy Carter, *Why Not the Best?* (Nashville, Tenn.: Broadman Press, 1975), p. 122.

18. Ethel Mendelsohn and John H. Galvin, "The Legal Status of Women," in *The Book of the States, 1978-1979* (Lexington, Ky.: Council of State Governments, 1978), p. 263.

2
CAMPAIGN TECHNIQUES AND COSTS

Three of the most significant changes in gubernatorial campaigning in the 1970s and 1980s compared with campaigning in the 1940s and 1950s are (1) the greatly increased cost of a gubernatorial campaign in all states, (2) the greatly increased use of television as a campaign technique, and (3) the widespread use of political consultants in gubernatorial campaigns. These three developments are related in that both consultants and television are expensive and tend to add substantially to the cost of campaigning. However, consultants and television do not explain all the increased costs since more money is also being spent on more traditional campaign techniques such as direct-mail advertising, billboards and radio, and on other new techniques such as telephone banks used in direct appeals to selected voters. While a part of the increased cost is due to inflation, the cost of campaigning in the last two decades is still considerably higher than in the 1940s and 1950s even after a correction is made for the inflation factor.

The campaign techniques used in modern gubernatorial campaigning are discussed in the first section of this chapter while the increased cost and the items for which the gubernatorial war chest is spent are covered in the second section. Both of these topics are among the most fascinating found in the study of gubernatorial politics and both are worthy of book-length treatments. However, each must be discussed here only in summary fashion.

Campaign Techniques

The techniques used by gubernatorial candidates vary considerably from state to state and even within a state with the passage of time and the changing personalities of the candidates. What is sure-fire campaigning in Alabama may be completely ineffectual in California. The answer to state and regional variations lies only in part in the old proverb that "you have to cut a garment in accordance to the cloth." For example, in the past the cloth in the South was largely homespun and had to be cut accordingly. However, the historical composition of the electorate now is only a part of the answer. The South is rapidly becoming industrialized and urbanized and thus is losing much of its old homespun flavor. If its politics remains highly personalized, it is due less to differences in the electorate than to the South's position still as a one-party Democratic enclave at the state level.

Recent developments in the southern states suggest that they are becoming more Republican. However, this developing Republicanism is only a relative term that must be understood as a gain by what is still a definite minority party in the Deep South. The trend over the past decade shows something of this growth but also confirms the Republicans' minority status, at least for the 1970s. For example, the Republicans entered the decade with only three Republican governors in the South. One of these was Winthrop Rockefeller (1967-71) who was completing his second two-year term in Arkansas. Another was Claude R. Kirk, Jr., of Florida (1967-71) who was completing his only term in that state. The third was Linwood Holton (1970-74) who had just taken office in January 1970 after having been elected in November 1969 as the first Republican governor of Virginia in modern times.

Rockefeller's original election in Arkansas in 1966 and his reelection in 1968 seems to have been based on personal popularity, aided and abetted by two of the most expensive gubernatorial campaigns in the state's history. The Republican success was not repeated in the 1970s since no Republicans were elected in that decade. However, the 1980s started with a victory for the GOP, since Frank D. White was elected governor in 1980 for a two-year term.

The Rockefeller magic in Arkansas did not spill over into the legislative ranks. The Republican percentage of the senate in that state ran from zero percent early in the decade to a high of 2.8 percent in 1978, a figure that was maintained in 1980. There were a few more Republicans in the house, totaling 5 percent in 1978; they increased to 7 percent in 1980, still not an impressive figure.

The Florida term of Claude R. Kirk, Jr., also proved to be an aberration for the 1970s. No Republican (as of 1980) has been elected governor since Kirk. However, the Republicans are gaining ground in the Florida legislature. The most recent figures show that they had 22.5 percent of the legislative seats in the senate in 1978 and 32.5 percent in 1980. The Republicans also did well in the house with 22.5 percent of the seats in 1978 and 32.5 percent in 1980. These percentages are the second highest in the South (see Table 8).

The recent Virginia habit of electing Republican governors seems to represent a significant political shift. Linwood Holton (1970–74) was followed by Mills E. Godwin, Jr. (1974–78), who in turn was

TABLE 8
THE PERCENTAGE OF SEATS HELD BY REPUBLICANS IN SOUTHERN LEGISLATURES, 1978-1980

State	Senate		House	
	1978	1980	1978	1980
Tennessee	27.3	36.4	32.3	39.3
Florida	22.5	32.5	22.5	32.5
Texas	12.9	22.6	12.7	24.0
Virginia	12.5	22.5	21.0	25.0
Georgia	7.1	8.9	13.3	12.8
South Carolina	6.5	10.9	9.7	13.7
North Carolina	6.0	20.0	5.0	20.0
Mississippi	3.8	7.7	2.4	3.3
Arkansas	2.8	2.8	5.0	7.0
Louisiana	2.6	0.0	3.8	9.5
Alabama	0.0	0.0	1.9	3.8

SOURCE: *The Book of the States, 1978–79* (Lexington, Ky.: Council of State Governments, 1978), p. 13, and *The Book of the States, 1980–81* (Lexington, Ky.: Council of State Governments, 1980), p. 85.

NOTE: The 1978 percentages are based on the composition of the legislatures in January 1978. The 1980 percentages reflect the changes caused by the 1978 and 1979 legislative elections.

succeeded by John N. Dalton (1978–). Thus, Virginia has had three Republican governors in succession, the largest number of any southern state in the 1970s. The Republicans also are increasing their strength in the Virginia Legislature. In 1978 the Republicans held 12.5 percent of the senate seats, but in 1980 this percentage almost doubled to 22.5 percent. In the house the percentage rose slightly from 21 percent in 1978 to 25 percent in 1980.

In 1970 a Republican, Winfield Dunn (1971–75), was elected governor of Tennessee. However, he was succeeded by a Democrat, Ray Blanton (1975–79). Governor Blanton in turn was succeeded by Lamar Alexander (1979–), the second Republican governor of the decade. Thus Republican governors were the dominant factor in gubernatorial politics for 60 percent of the period under discussion. Tennessee also had a substantial Republican legislative delegation since the Senate was 36.4 percent Republican in 1980 and the House 39.3 percent. Because Tennessee was one of the eleven states in the Confederacy, it has long been considered a "southern" state. However, its politics in recent years has been more like that of the border states which, of course, is what Tennessee is in geographic terms. Certainly it cannot be considered a one-party Democratic state as was the case in the 1930s, 1940s, and 1950s, and it may be moving towards a genuine two-party status.

The latest Republican gubernatorial triumph in the South was the election of David C. Treen in 1979 as the first Republican governor of Louisiana since Reconstruction. Treen, however, faces an overwhelmingly Democratic legislature since no Republican senators were elected in 1979. The house is a little more encouraging, but even here there are only 10 Republicans out of a house of 105 members, hardly a very impressive bloc with which to work.

The election of a respectable number of Republican governors and the increase in the number of Republican legislators are legitimate cause for self-congratulation among southern Republicans. However, these developments have not produced substantial legislative blocs except in Tennessee, Florida, and Virginia. Consequently, in spite of the improved showing of the Republicans in recent gubernatorial and legislative elections, real party organizations complete with ward clubs, precinct captains, and paid party workers who assiduously push door bells still are virtually unknown in the South. Hence, neither party has a latent organization which need only be activated to swing into action behind a candidate. Furthermore, the Democratic party ordinarily does not use the machinery that it does have to support a candidate in the Democratic primary where the crucial battle is still fought in most southern states. As a consequence, politics, while everywhere a highly individualistic art, is even more personalized in the one-party South than in other sections of the country. In the primary campaign each candidate is thrown on his own resources and must build whatever organization he deems necessary from the ground up. Under these circumstances it is not surprising that candidates resort to some sort of gimmick to make them stand out from the field.

Over thirty years ago Ellis Arnall, the liberal former governor of Georgia, well summarized the necessity for this sort of campaign. Arnall had been asked in an interview to comment on the use of the Strawberry Pickers, a tireless aggregation of country musicians with whom Big Jim Folsom had successfully stumped the state of Alabama in the 1946 gubernatorial campaign. According to Arnall, "It was necessary for Folsom to use color and showmanship to win the governorship. The parlor liberals and advocates of good government in every state must realize that you have to have some showmanship and be a politician before you can develop into a statesman."[1]

Gubernatorial campaigns in the South have not changed appreciably in mood in the thirty years since Governor Arnall gave his analysis of the Folsom campaign, but they have become much more sophisticated in method and technique, particularly in the greater use of radio and television. Nevertheless, the problem of being elected governor in a one-party Democratic state in the 1980s is still the same as it was in the 1940s. Name recognition is crucial in a one-party primary. Hence, as Governor Arnall said, a candidate must first be a politician and be elected before he can become a statesman. It should be stressed that in most of the South a candidate must be a politician and be nominated in the Democratic primary before he can be a candidate in the general election and finally be elected. Also, it is still true that in a one-party state, in normally Democratic or Republican states and, to an increasing extent in two-party states, the candidate is strictly on his own in the primary. Since there are few clear-cut issues but many candidates in the average primary, the appeal to the voter tends to become based on personality. Hence, many forces are at work to impel candidates to try to attract attention by what they do rather than by what they think.

The difference between the electoral process in one-party states and that found in the two-party states or in the normally Democratic or normally Republican categories lies not in the primary but in the general election. In the more competitive states, while personalities also tend to obscure issues, the successful candidate in the primary may expect party support in the general election and hence is not entirely on his own in his attempt to win the governorship. The race for the governorship probably will not be decided until the general election, where the voting will reflect party discipline, a factor unknown in the one-party Democratic states. In the competitive states where the governor may expect some support from his party in the general election, the kind of campaign which he wages may be tempered to fit party policies. However, it will probably be dictated in large measure by the candidate's past political experience, the political exigencies of the moment, the advice of his political consultant, and by his own personality.

The particular focus taken by a campaign or the gimmick used are as varied as the gubernatorial candidates and the political consultants whom they hire. Many of the methods used such as direct mail advertising or television are fairly standard and are discussed in the next section of this chapter as part of campaign finance. However, there are many campaigns built around a central theme that may or may not be issue-oriented. A good example of this type of campaign was the 1978 "workingman's campaign" waged by Democratic candidate Robert "Bob" Graham in Florida. In order to make himself stand out from the crowd he adopted the idea of working a full day at each of 100 different jobs. His campaign slogan was "Bob Graham—Working for Governor." These working days were covered by the press on many occasions. To ensure that these efforts were recorded, many of them were made into television commercials featuring shots of Graham collecting garbage or herding dairy cows. It is difficult to assess the impact of this particular strategy. However, this campaign is a good example of how the modern media and a suggestion from a political consultant can be parlayed into the kind of coverage that becomes a significant factor in the name recognition which is essential in a crowded field such as was found in Florida in 1978. Since "Working Bob" is now Governor Robert Graham, it is fair to assume that the strategy worked.

It should be pointed out, however, that in political campaigning, as in most human endeavors, there is not much that is really new. The idea so effective in Florida in 1978 had been used previously for the equally successful campaign of Cliff Finch for governor of Mississippi in 1975.[2]

"Gimmick" campaigns are by no means limited to the normally Democratic states in the South. On the contrary, they seem to be spreading rapidly to all parts of the country. For example, in Illinois in 1972 Daniel Walker, who was subsequently elected governor of that state, waged a campaign featuring a highly publicized walk across the state. The same technique was used by Joseph Teasdale in his unsuccessful campaign for governor of Missouri in 1972. Teasdale, who became known as "Walking Joe" because of this effort, won in a subsequent attempt in 1976 against incumbent Governor Kit Bond. His second race appeared to be more issue oriented, but it seems probable that the name recognition from his previous unsuccessful campaign was a factor in his subsequent election.

Former President Jimmy Carter, who was then gubernatorial candidate Carter, in his second try for the Georgia governorship in 1970 waged a campaign that featured a person-to-person approach. As President Carter later explained it, he and Rosalynn shook hands over a four-year period with half of the voters in Georgia.[3]

It should not be assumed, because a candidate has a gimmick or concentrates on a particular campaign technique, that the standard campaign methods are not used. If the voters are not "told" via the press or if they are not "shown" how hard a candidate is "working" or "walking," the impact of his gimmick is limited to those whom he contacts personally. Therefore, these activities are highly publicized in the press, and on radio and television. For any type of gubernatorial campaign, with or without a gimmick, radio and television have now become two of the most important methods of campaigning. The blessings that the electronic media have brought to gubernatorial campaigning are not unmixed. Although both radio and television are effective when skillfully utilized, they also are very expensive and may tend to give some advantage to the individual who can afford to buy the most time on the air.

Radio has been used for many years as a part of the campaign techniques of most gubernatorial candidates, and it is still widely used although television is cutting into its popularity in most states. However, on strictly a cost basis, radio does seem to be particularly effective in achieving name recognition for a candidate who has not previously been in politics or who seeks to move up from a minor post such as that of a state legislator. For example, in the Alabama gubernatorial campaign of 1978 one of the candidates was Fob James, a self-made businessman who had not previously run for public office of any kind. Public opinion polls conducted early in the race showed that James definitely had a difficult recognition problem. In fact, only eight months before the first primary he ranked last of all the Democratic candidates in name recognition. However, millionaire James poured a flood of dollars into both radio and television spots over the eight months just prior to the first primary. Some observers credit his unexpectedly good showing in the first primary to this media blitz, particularly his radio spots over local stations in rural areas. These spots plus short television plugs apparently brought him to the attention of enough of the state's voters to make him a statewide personality and propel him into a runoff against Attorney General Bill Baxley, who was a well known political figure in the state. James won the runoff against Baxley and subsequently was elected governor over only token Republican opposition. While the recognition factor is important in any gubernatorial election, it is especially important when the candidate is running against established political figures who are well known in the state as were all three of James's opponents. At least a part of James's success must be attributed to his short but numerous radio and television spots, which had catchy, tuneful "jingles" as a major ingredient.

Although television is a more recent development than radio in gubernatorial campaigning, it is now absolutely vital in most states. This is particularly true of states such as California with its large area and huge population. For example, Robert Pack, in a recent study of California Governor Jerry Brown, concluded that Brown relied very little on the Democratic party in his races. Rather, he made extremely vigorous attempts to reach the voters directly via the news media,[4] attempts that have been successful since Brown has won three statewide elections in California including two for the governorship.

Pack's conclusions are supported by the author's interviews in California. In fact, one interviewee, in what definitely was not intended to be a derogatory comment, said that the governor was "created" by television. This perhaps is putting the matter too strongly, but the point is that in a huge state with widely dispersed concentrations of population, the use of television is an absolute necessity. In order to impress upon his listener the population differential, the staffer said that there were several state senatorial districts in California that had more people to be represented than were represented by United States senators from several smaller states. Interesting enough, there are several senate districts in which a state senator in California represents more persons in the state senate than both United States senators from several smaller states represent in the United States Senate. In fact, if the California senate had been apportioned strictly in accordance with population in 1970, the average state senate district would have contained more people than that of the three smallest states. In California the 1970 population was approximately 19,953,000 and the state senate had 40 senators. Thus, had the senate districts been exactly even in population in 1970, each senator would have represented 498,825 persons. In Vermont, Wyoming, and Alaska, the three states with the smallest populations in 1970, both United States senators from those states would have represented only 444,732, 332,416, and 302,173 persons respectively, because those figures represent the total population of those states.

The point of this comparison is not to raise the old argument of population versus area as a basis for representation but to emphasize the fact that to reach what is now (in 1980) well over 23 million people, a gubernatorial candidate in California must use the media, especially television, effectively. The view expressed here of the importance of the media in California is supported by a poll taken after the 1974 election in which four out of ten California voters interviewed said that advertising (not including direct mail) was the most effective campaign technique in that state. Thus, both citizens and political observers seem to have the same concept of the importance of "selling" the candidate in California.

The same line of reasoning seems to apply to other states as well. As is shown by the figures in the next section, television generally ranks first and radio second in campaign spending. While it is not entirely true that candidates are packaged and sold like cereal, there is much truth in this popular assumption. Those who direct gubernatorial campaigns apparently believe that the television, radio, and newspaper blitz produces results. If this were not the case, it seems unlikely that all the candidates would use the media to the limit of their financial resources as is apparently the case.

No comment on the media would be complete without emphasizing the fact that print media is still used in all campaigns. However, because of the importance of radio and television, the print media do not command the undivided attention of candidates as was once the case. Print media, at least the newspaper portion of it, also differ from much of radio and television in that most newspapers endorse the candidate of their choice in gubernatorial races. While editorial support is generally welcomed by a candidate, actually it probably is not as important in a campaign as daily coverage by a newspaper of what a candidate says and does. Newspapers can easily push their favored candidate by covering as front page "news" anything he does during his campaign. While the activities of his opponent, or opponents if the election is a primary, also will be covered, the coverage can be less extensive and the stories less prominently placed in the paper.

The importance of the print media varies from campaign to campaign but in general it now seems to trail television and radio, at least in the amount of money spent on it. Nevertheless, many candidates who grew up when the print media predominated frequently have trouble adjusting to the other forms of media coverage. A good example of this problem, although in an unusually extreme form, happened during the 1978 gubernatorial race in New York. Because of the newspaper pressmen's strike, New York's three major daily newspapers were all shut down just one month before the September primary. This "news blackout" lasted for the *Times* and the *Daily News* until November 6, one day before the election. The *Post,* which was an afternoon paper, was able to get back in print by late September, but it did not reach all those who would normally be reached by the other two papers. Governor Hugh

Carey apparently was able to adjust his campaign more satisfactorily than that of his opponent, Assembly Minority Leader Perry Duryea, who originally had a twenty-point lead in the polls. Carey used visual items that could be covered easily on television and received a great deal of television coverage. Perhaps one of his best unpaid television "spots" was shown during a nightly newscast which featured Governor Carey helping stock a lake in Central Park with catfish. This episode made excellent picture coverage since it showed Governor Carey, with his shirt-sleeves rolled up, throwing catfish into the lake and baiting fishhooks for children. In other words, Carey was able to adjust to the newspaper strike whereas his opponent apparently could not.

In concluding this discussion on campaign techniques, it should be pointed out that most gubernatorial candidates now employ political consultants to assist them in planning and conducting their campaigns. These consultants come in many sizes and varieties, but three of the best known at the gubernatorial level are David Garth, Robert Squier, and Deloss Walker. Garth ran the successful campaigns of John Gilligan in Ohio, Brendan Byrne in New Jersey, and Hugh Carey in New York, while Squier handled John Y. Brown's winning campaign in Kentucky and Bob Graham's successful effort in Florida. Deloss Walker is perhaps not as well known nationally as the other two, but he has been very successful in the South. Walker handled Fob James's successful campaign in Alabama and those of Dolph Briscoe in Texas and William L. Waller in Mississippi.

The use of political consultants is not a new development in political campaigning but, because of the importance of the media in campaigns, their use has become much more widespread. Thus, while political consultants probably have increased the effectiveness of gubernatorial campaigning, they have also increased its cost. The amount a consultant charges for his services is a confidential matter and is generally not revealed by a candidate unless the state's campaign finance law requires such a listing. The fee that the political consultant receives depends in large measure on how much he does in a campaign. For example, a consultant might charge $25,000 a month if he handled the entire campaign but only $10,000 a month, plus commissions on advertising, if he handled only the advertising in a campaign. In the general election in New Jersey in 1977, the winning candidate listed $180,000 for "advertising production and consulting." This listing makes it difficult to separate the two, but it probably is sound to assume that a major part of this went for "consulting" since radio, television, and newspaper advertising were listed separately.

Each consultant has his own formula for the amount to be devoted to advertising in a campaign. For example, one consultant felt that at least two-thirds of the expenditures made by a candidate should go to media advertising. However, his definition of the media is very broad and includes not only radio, television, and the newspapers but also magazines, bus cards, billboards, and the cost of persons on street corners distributing flyers. The reason for this emphasis on every conceivable form of advertising is that information about the candidate must be conveyed to every potential voter. Since in most campaigns for governor there are simply too many people for the candidate to contact personally, all avenues to the voter must be exploited.

Another consultant (Deloss Walker) is quoted as saying that "The most important thing in a campaign is honesty, you can't really fool the public and so pat 'formulas' don't work. What I try to do in a campaign is portray a person as he or she is and to show the voter that the candidate is someone they can trust."[5]

One political observer felt that the gubernatorial campaigns in 1978 in Alabama definitely showed the influence of the new breed of political consultant. He noted that the campaign marked " . . . the passing of the old-style, barnstorming methods of the past. Gone, or at least cast into strictly secondary roles, are the mass rallies, the firebrand stump speeches and the door-to-door canvassing of elections past."[6]

There definitely has been a distinct shift to media-centered campaigns not only in Alabama and in the South but in gubernatorial campaigning in general. However, perhaps it is too early to discard entirely the methods of the past, especially in states with rural traditions and small populations. While it is true that stylized billboards, snappy slogans, radio jingles, and the omnipresent television spots are extremely important in selling the candidate, there are still some occasions in which old-time campaigning, especially "pressing the flesh," is still important. For example, in the race in New Mexico in 1979 Democrat Bruce King narrowly defeated Republican Joe Skeen by a margin of fewer than 4,000 votes out of the nearly 350,000 cast. At the close of this race, Governor King was quoted as saying that he had probably shaken hands with two-thirds of the voters in the state. Thus, in smaller states such as New Mexico, even though the latest in media techniques may be used, shaking hands may still be a very important factor in a close race.

Campaign Costs

The problem of determining what it costs to become governor has been made less difficult in recent years because of new state legislation regulating campaign expenditures and requiring more accurate reporting of them. However, the drive for more complete public control of campaigning received a setback in 1976 when the U.S. Supreme Court in *Buckley v. Valeo* held that overall limits on campaign costs and restrictions on the amounts candidates themselves can spend were so intimately related to freedom of speech that a limit on spending was a limit on freedom of expression and hence unconstitutional.[7] Fortunately, the same decision did uphold the concept of public disclosure and limits on candidates who accepted public funds.

Nevertheless, the constitutionality of many of the laws in the twenty-two states still having overall campaign limits is now in question. In eleven states the limits appear to be clearly unconstitutional since they provide for an overall limit on all expenditures for a candidate. In the other eleven states some of the laws may stand since they provide for limits for an "authorized" campaign committee. In some of these eleven, however, the law also specifies a limit on spending by the candidate himself, and that limit seems clearly to be contrary to the Valeo decision.

Even if we assume the constitutionality of the limits in some states and the good faith of the candidate in abiding by them, we still may not get a complete picture of campaign finance. Obviously, the expenditures of the candidate himself form only a small part of total campaign spending. In addition, the expenditures of even "authorized" campaign committees do not account for all funds spent. The figures quoted in this section, therefore, are in most cases estimates based on the best information which could be obtained through interviews or from written sources.

The cost of campaigning varies from state to state and also from election to election within the same state because of such factors as the quality of the opposition, the presence of real issues in the campaign, the political following with which a given candidate starts the race, and, particularly in the case of a person of great personal wealth, the amount of money the candidate has at his disposal. State-to-state variations are also caused by the type of party and/or factional political organization in the state, the importance of the primary, the geographical configuration of the state, and the size of the electorate.

It would seem logical that the cost of campaigning in most two-party states should be greater than in one-party states of comparable size and population because of the necessity for conducting two campaigns, one in the primary to secure the nomination and another in the general election. While this is probably true in some cases, such is the variation from campaign to campaign caused by the other factors listed above that it is difficult to document this logic. Furthermore, in nine one-party states we find the double primary system that forces the two most successful candidates to conduct two campaigns, one in the first primary and one in the runoff primary. This feature, together with the fact that factional politics places a premium on campaigning and showmanship, seems to make the cost of campaigning in the South as expensive as in two-party states of comparable area and population.

In view of all these variations, average figures on the cost of campaigning for governor are relatively meaningless. Indeed, when a wealthy man is running, estimates which would be "reasonable" under normal circumstances suddenly become entirely inadequate. For example, in the 1970s the cost of the winning campaigns for governor in Alabama seldom exceeded $1 million for both the primary and general election. However, in the 1978 campaign, one Democratic candidate, Fob James, reported that he spent some $3.6 million in the first primary and in the runoff. More than half of this total went for campaign advertising. His chief opponent, Attorney General Bill Baxley, reported spending $1.2 million in the two primaries. Thus, the 1978 gubernatorial race in Alabama, even before the general election, was the most costly in the state's history.[8] In the runoff primary, James defeated Baxley for the Democratic nomination and went on to win the governorship in the ensuing general election.

The pattern was much the same in the Democratic primary held in Tennessee in the summer of 1978 when almost $5 million was spent in the primary. The winner, Jack E. (Jake) Butcher, spent $2.2 million in the campaign, which was almost as much as the combined spending of his three opponents. On the Republican side, Lamar Alexander spent only $672,940 in a much less hotly contested race for the Republican nomination. The ensuing general election was also a free-spending affair with Butcher spending something in the neighborhood of $2.5 million and Alexander slightly over $1 million.[9] However, in spite of his greater expenditures Butcher lost to Alexander by some 100,000 votes to return the governorship to the Republicans.

Another example of a free-spending race was the 1977 Democratic primary in Virginia where the two top contenders were Henry Howell and Andrew Miller. Howell spent a reported $566,000 while his opponent spent an estimated $1,042,000. Thus Miller outspent Howell by almost two to one but still managed to lose the primary. The general election was another matter, however. Howell was apparently still underfinanced since he spent only $777,000 compared to $1,863,000 spent by his Republican opponent, John N. Dalton, who had been nominated in the Republican convention.[10] Howell lost to Dalton, and the loss must be attributed at least in part to the tremendous edge in spending by the Republican candidate.

Perhaps the most costly gubernatorial election in recent years was the 1979 gubernatorial contest in Louisiana. In that election the six principal candidates spent over $20 million in both the primary and the general election in what appears to have been the highest total in the nation in recent elections.

The two candidates who emerged as victors in the Louisiana version of the nonpartisan primary were David Treen (a Republican) and Louis Lambert (a Democrat). In the primary Treen spent $2.5 million to come in first while Lambert spent an even higher $3.2 million for his second place finish. In addition, the other candidates spent another $10 million on their losing efforts. Thus, the total cost of the primary was an astronomical $16 million. In the ensuing general election Treen outspent Lambert by more than two to one ($3.2 million to $1.5 million) to add another $4.7 million to the cost of running for governor. Treen won the race both in terms of expenditures made and in votes obtained. However, his electoral margin was extremely close since he won by only 9,557 votes out of more than 1,371,825 votes cast, or less than six-tenths of a percentage point. Some idea of the magnitude of the spending in the 1979 Louisiana election may be seen by a comparison with the 1976 election in New York. In that election the total spent in the primary and general election was about $13,247,000 compared to $20,600,000 in Louisiana. Of course, the cost per vote in New York was much less because of the larger electoral turnout there, only $2.26 per vote compared to $7.73 for Louisiana.

While the 1979 dollar total in Louisiana seems to be the largest in a gubernatorial race in recent history, it does not quite win the cost per vote derby. That distinction, as of 1979, belongs to Alaska whose last gubernatorial election cost the two candidates a staggering $19.01 per vote cast. The dollar total of about $2,400,000 did not even come close to that of Louisiana where the winning candidate alone spent $3,277,000 or about $877,000 more than both candidates in Alaska.[11]

There are "rich man" races from time to time in some states with smaller populations, in which millions are spent on gubernatorial contests. However, on the average, gubernatorial campaigns in the more populous states generally cost the most money, although, as was suggested in the case of Louisiana, the campaigns in larger states frequently are not as expensive if figured on a cost per vote basis. Some fairly typical figures in 1977 and 1978 were the campaigns in New Jersey, Michigan, Minnesota, and Massachusetts. These states varied widely in geographic location, one being Middle Atlantic, one East North Central, one West North Central, and another in New England. They are somewhat closer to each other in population with New Jersey ranking eighth (7,168,000 in 1970), Michigan seventh (8,875,000), Massachusetts tenth (5,689,000), while Minnesota has the smallest population with only 3,805,000 persons in 1970 to give it a ranking of nineteenth in the nation.

The political patterns of the four are also different and have shifted in three of them over the past decade. For example, during the period 1961–70 New Jersey was a normally Democratic state while Michigan was at the other end of the spectrum, being normally Republican. Massachusetts fell in the two-party category, while Minnesota could not be classified in any category. It had a nonpartisan legislature, although it elected two Republican governors to only one Democratic govenor during this period.

In more recent years (1972–80), the situation changed somewhat. Minnesota abandoned its nonpartisan legislature in 1972, and both the house and senate were Democratic-Farmer-Labor for the remainder of the decade. During the first eight years of the period Minnesota also had a Democratic-Farmer-Labor governor. However, in the gubernatorial election of 1978, Republican Albert H. Quie was elected governor.

Massachusetts in the last ten years has moved over to the Democratic column to become a normally Democratic state, thus joining New Jersey, which remained in that category. Michigan also has shifted, moving out of the normally Republican group into the two-party category. Thus, the political party pattern in the four states as of 1980 was fairly representative of the varying kinds of party patterns found in the states as a whole.[12]

Because of these variations in geographic location, population, and party control, these states make interesting subjects for comparison. In addition, they all have in common some form of public financing for their gubernatorial campaigns, although the details of the plans vary widely as does the amount of money actually given to each candidate. In New Jersey in 1977 the Democratic candidate Brendan T. Byrne spent roughly $1,667,000 in the general election of which $1,051,000 was public money. His Republican opponent Raymond H. Bateman spent $1,642,000 with $1,020,000 in public funding. The Michigan campaign in 1978 cost the winner, Republican William G. Milliken, $1,143,000, while the Democratic candidate William Fitzgerald spent $1,102,000 in a losing cause. Both candidates received a flat amount, $750,000, for their respective campaigns.

The Minnesota race saw Albert Quie win as the Republican candidate with an expenditure of $1,062,000, while the loser Rudy Perpich spent $565,000 of which $190,000 came from state funds. It should be noted that Quie did not accept public financing in this campaign. Consequently, he was not bound by the $600,000 spending limit established by statute in Minnesota for any candidate who accepts public financing. Quie actually spent $462,000 more than his limit would have been had he accepted public financing and almost twice as much as the losing Democratic candidate.

The gubernatorial candidates in Massachusetts got the least help from the state of any candidates in the four races. Massachusetts has a plan under which the taxpayer can designate a part of his taxes for political campaigns. However, in 1977 this plan raised less than $100,000, which had to cover both the primaries and the general election not only of the governor but also of several other state-wide officers. The result is that each candidate received only $13,000 in public funding. This was a drop in the bucket in a campaign in which the Democratic candidate Edward J. King spent $793,000 to win the election over Republican Francis W. Hatch, who spent $676,000.[13]

Not all big spenders are the winners, but this is true more often than not in the general election. Where the correlation seems to break down is in the primary, particularly in the primary of the party out of power. In such a primary, when a group of well-financed candidates vie to be their party's nominee so that they can take on the incumbent governor, large sums of money are spent with what appears to be little effect. For example, in the Republican primary in California in 1978 over $6 million was spent by the contestants just for the right to run against the incumbent Democratic Governor Jerry Brown, who did not appear to be particularly vulnerable. The major Republican candidate in terms of the amount of money spent in the primary was former Los Angeles Police Chief Ed Davis. While Davis finished second in the primary, he did manage to raise and spend some $1.8 million, more than any of his competitors in the Republican ranks.[14] The winner of the Republican primary was Evelle Younger who lost to Brown in the ensuing general election by over 1 million votes.

In the 1976 gubernatorial race in Missouri, incumbent Governor Christopher (Kit) Bond had no real opposition in the Republican primary but nevertheless spent $243,673 in his bid for renomination. On the other hand, State Senator Joseph P. Teasdale had substantial opposition in the Democratic primary from State Senator

William J. Cason. In this primary Teasdale spent $161,876 while Cason spent $414,221. However, in this case money apparently was not the deciding factor since Teasdale beat Cason in the primary. Thus, the stage was set for confrontation between Bond and Teasdale. Teasdale pulled one of the surprising upsets of the 1976 gubernatorial elections by beating Bond in the general election. In that election Bond spent a reported $273,718 while Teasdale spent $649,976. Thus, Teasdale spent a total of $811,852 in the primary and general election while Bond spent a total of $517,391.[15] In seeking explanations for Teasdale's success, several local papers attributed it to his aggressive television campaign. In addition, at least one paper quoted unidentified former backers of Teasdale as saying that television was a major factor in his primary victory over William J. Cason. Since both of the candidates spent about the same amount on television and radio (in the neighborhood of $330,000 each), it may have been either what the candidates said on television, the quality of their television spots, or the timing of their television campaign that made the difference. For example, it appears that Teasdale spent most of his television budget in the closing days of the campaign. This timing may have been crucial to his success. While neither he nor his opponent commented directly on this point, Governor Bond at a news conference shortly after his defeat is quoted as saying that he wished he had spent more on mass media.[16]

While it is not entirely clear just how many persons actually do watch political ads on television, the odds seem to be in favor of substantial exposure for the candidate if he sticks to short commercial length "spots." Such spot advertising is woven into the regular program in the same fashion as are ads for soft drinks, antacids, automobiles, beer, cosmetics, and a host of products whose manufacturers spend millions each year in attempting to reach the American public via radio and television. Robert J. Gwyn explains the impact of this advertising:

> The broadcast media are a part of most Americans' lives. The statistics on the media are staggering: the United States has more radio sets than people (425 million sets, 216 million people). Nearly 72 million homes (97 percent of all American homes) have television sets

and the A. C. Neilsen Company, a principal media polling service, reports that in over 63 percent of these homes the set is turned on in the evening. In the average American home the set is on over six hours a day.

A radio audience study reports that the total radio audience in each twenty-four hour period is nearly 24 million people over the age of twelve. Most communities have more radio stations than daily newspapers and large cities have more television stations than daily newspapers.[17]

Even the fiftieth state does not appear to be immune from the high cost of gubernatorial campaigning. Although Hawaii had only about 770,000 people in 1970, the cost of the winning 1970 gubernatorial campaign was $972,000. In a sharp primary fight, incumbent Governor John A. Burns spent $697,000 to beat back the challenge of Thomas P. Gill, who spent another $205,000. However, the cost per vote was astronomical since Burns received only 82,400 votes for a cost of $8.46 a vote while Gill spent $2.97 for each of his 69,000 votes. The Republican primary was not as costly but, even so, the winner Samuel P. King managed to spend $274,000.

In the thirty-one day general election campaign, Burns spent another $275,000, but was slightly outspent in this race by King who spent $278,000. Thus, if we consider the money spent in both the primary and general election by each candidate, we find that Burns, the winner, spent slightly over $7.05 per vote for each of the 137,800 votes he received in the general election, while King spent about $5.45 for each of his 101,200 votes.[18]

The 1970 campaign was noteworthy not only for its spending but for its introduction of big time television advertising, the use of public opinion polls, political consultants, and all of the other paraphernalia of mainland campaigning to Hawaiian politics. The television campaign used by the Burns camp was so good that a year after the campaign a collage of the campaign films won an award for political advertising at an international film festival. One observer, in commenting on the election, said that "For old-fashioned canvassing, for political polling, for advertising consultation, and for television programming probably more money was spent per vote than in any previous election in the country."[19]

A survey of the other races involving large-scale spending in the 1970 gubernatorial campaigns supports this observation at least for the 1970 election. There were ten gubernatorial candidates who spent $1 million or more in their campaigns, and nine of these ten candidates won their races. However, none of them matched the expenditures of John Burns on a cost per vote basis.

The three candidates with million-dollar campaigns in states whose politics most closely approximated the political situation in Hawaii in 1970 were Alabama, Arkansas, and Georgia. All three of these states normally have a habit of electing Democrats as governors, and in all of them the real race for governor is normally in the Democratic primary. All are considerably larger in population than Hawaii, and all have a larger turnout of voters. However, their size and voter turnout does not substantially alter the spending patterns in their gubernatorial campaigns. For example, in the 1970 gubernatorial year, when John Burns spent $972,000 in Hawaii, George Wallace spent over $1 million in Alabama. As was the case in Hawaii, the spending in Alabama was concentrated in the Democratic primary where Wallace spent about $930,000; he spent only an additional $96,000 in the general election, which is a more pro forma event in Alabama than in Hawaii. For a state its size, voter turnout in Alabama in the general election is small, and Wallace polled only 636,975 votes for his victory at a total cost per vote for primary plus the general election of $1.60 per vote.

Much the same pattern of spending usually is found in Arkansas since it is essentially a one-party Democratic state. However, in 1970 there was an atypical situation there since the incumbent governor, Winthrop Rockefeller, was a Republican. Consequently, in the 1970 election the candidates spent more in the general election than in the primary. Rockefeller's Democratic opponent, Dale Bumpers, spent $180,000 in the Democratic primary and $293,679 in the general election for a total of $473,679 or a modest $1.26 per vote in a winning effort. The loser, Winthrop Rockefeller, spent only $60,000 in a lightly contested Republican primary. However, he spent a whopping $1,314,162 in the general election for a total cost of $6.96 per general election vote, almost as great as John Burns's $7.05 in Hawaii. In contrast, Jimmy Carter, in winning in one-party Georgia in the same year, spent $1 million in the Democratic primary, but only $240,000 in the general election for a total cost in the general election of $2.02 per vote.

Two other relationships were explored in order to get additional comparisons of John Burns's spending in Hawaii with that of candidates in other states in the 1970 gubernatorial races. The first of these was a comparison of the Burns cost per vote with the amount per vote spent by the winning gubernatorial candidate in Alaska in the 1970 race on the chance that the states might have something in common since they were the two states most recently admitted. However, the states actually proved to have little else in common. Not only do they have well-known differences in climate, but most other significant characteristics also seem to be different. For example, Hawaii's 1970 population of 769,000 ranked fortieth among the states compared to Alaska's 302,000 persons and fiftieth ranking. Alaska was only 48.4 percent urban, while Hawaii was 83.1 percent urban. Hawaii had a population density of 119.8, while Alaska, because of its vast size, showed the lowest population density in the nation with only 0.5 persons per square mile. The politics of the two states also are different. Hawaii, since statehood, has been predominantly Democratic while Alaska, though normally Democratic in the 1960s, became a two-party state in the 1970s.

This difference is reflected in party control of the governorship in each state. In Hawaii William F. Quinn, a Republican who had been the presidentially appointed governor from 1957 to 1959, was elected as the state's first governor for a shortened term in 1959 and served until 1962. He was succeeded by John A. Burns, a Democrat, who was elected to three successive terms in 1962, in 1966, and in 1970. Burns was succeeded in 1974 by his Democratic protégé, George R. Ariyoshi, who was reelected in 1978.

Alaska, on the other hand, moved from normally Democratic status prior to 1970 to a two-party status in the last ten years. In the first year of statehood, William A. Egan, a Democrat, was elected governor in 1959 for an abbreviated term. He was succeeded by Republican Walter J. Hickel for one term but returned to the governor's chair for another four-year term in the election of 1970.[20] In 1974 he was replaced by Republican Jay Hammond, who was reelected in 1978.

The winning percentage of the major party vote also has been different in the two states. In Hawaii the Democratic party's percentage of the two-party vote was 57.6 in 1970, 54.6 in 1974, and 55.2 in 1978. The races in Alaska have been much closer with the winning Democratic percentage in 1970 being 52.4 while the Republicans polled only 50.2 percent of the vote in 1974. In the 1974 race the Republican gubernatorial candidate, Jay Hammond, won by the razor-thin margin of only 278 votes. In 1978 Governor Hammond had a hard fight in both the primary and the general election although he finally won in a three-way race with only 39.1 percent of the vote.

One thing the two states did have in common in 1970 was a relatively high cost per vote for the winning candidates. In Alaska in 1970 the winning candidate was Democrat William Egan, who had a very substantial cost per vote of $4.07 in the general election. Although Egan spent only a total of $173,000 in the primary and general election, compared to Burns's expenditures of $972,000, the small turnout of voters in sparsely populated Alaska resulted in Egan's winning the election with slightly over 42,000 votes to boost his cost to $4.07 per vote. This put him third in the cost per vote sweepstakes after Burns's $7.05 in Hawaii and Winthrop Rockefeller's $6.96 in Arkansas.

Another approach to the cost per vote question is to take those states most nearly equal to Hawaii in population and compare the winning campaigns in those states in 1970 with that in Hawaii. The comparable states would be those which in 1970 ranked just above and just below Hawaii in population. These include Maine (38th), Rhode Island (39th), New Hampshire (42d), and Idaho (43d). Hawaii (40th) ranks in the middle of this group while the District of Columbia (41st) is not a state.

Using this breakdown by population we find that in Maine the Democratic candidate won with an expenditure of $1.14 per vote, almost all of which was spent in the general election. In Rhode Island expenditures also were concentrated in the general election. In a close race the winning Democrat received only 50.1 percent of the vote, yet still spent only $2.08 per general election vote. In New Hampshire the Republican winner spent only $0.77 per vote while in Idaho the successful Democrat spent an even lower $0.47 for each Democratic ballot cast.

What these figures show is that, if a comparison is made between Hawaii and other states based either on other expensive campaigns in states of a strongly Democratic bent or on campaigns in states of comparable size regardless of political configuration, the results still put Hawaii at the top of the cost per vote list. Burns in 1970 clearly was the winner in the spending race with $7.05 per vote compared to Winthrop Rockefeller's $6.96, William Egan's $4.07, Jimmy Carter's $2.02 and George Wallace's $1.60. Of course, none of these candidates even came close to the $6,786,427 spent by Nelson A. Rockefeller in New York. However, because of the greater turnout of voters, Rockefeller averaged only a comparatively modest $2.15 for each vote that he attracted in the general election.[21]

The danger of using any one election year even as an illustration of the cost of running for governor is shown by an examination of the situation in Hawaii and Alaska only two elections later. In the election of 1978 the positions of the two states were reversed, and Alaska far outstripped Hawaii in the cost per vote battle. George Ariyoshi, the Democratic incumbent in Hawaii, spent a very sizable $1.9 million in the primary and general election. The pattern of spending was the same as it was in 1970. In his successful bid for reelection, Ariyoshi spent some $1.4 million in the 1978 primary but only $500,000 in the general election. His total expenditure of $1.9 million, however, translates into $12.67 for each vote for him in the general election.

On the other hand, in Alaska in the same election year the winner, Jay S. Hammond, spent $740,611 in garnering 49,580 votes in the general election at a cost of $14.93 per vote. His Democratic opponent, Chaney Croft, spent over one-half as much—$474,281— but drew only 25,656 votes for an even higher $18.48 per vote total. Both the official candidates of the two major parties thus spent more per vote than did Governor Ariyoshi in his race in 1978 in Hawaii. The Alaska race of 1978 was the costliest gubernatorial race on a cost per vote basis of all the races analyzed including those of 1980.[22]

The device used in this section of cost per vote for gubernatorial races is a useful comparative tool. However, it is not without its drawbacks as the figures quoted above illustrate. If only the costs in the general election are used in calculating the cost per vote, the key role of the primary in the one-party Democratic states is ignored. Thus, it seems only logical to include both primary and general election costs for two reasons. In the first place, a gubernatorial candidate must first be nominated before he can be elected; consequently, what it costs a candidate to become governor in a particular election must realistically include what was spent in the primary as well as the general election. In the second place, in the solidly Democratic states the primary is still the election. The big fight in Alabama in 1970 was in the Democratic primary; Wallace spent $930,000 in the primary as opposed to only $96,000 in the general election. The same pattern still prevailed two elections later in 1978 when Fob James spent over $3.5 million in the double primaries used in Alabama. Even in normally Democratic states such as Hawaii, the pattern is still very much the same with Burns spending almost two and one-half times as much in the primary as in the general election in 1970, and Ariyoshi spending over three and one-half times as much in 1978.

Arkansas in 1970 was an exception to the general spending pattern in that state since both candidates spent more in the general election than in the primary. This change was due to the presence of a strong Republican candidate in incumbent Governor Winthrop Rockefeller, who had won the governor's race in 1966 and in 1968. He proved to be a two-term phenomenon, however, since he lost to Democrat Dale Bumpers in 1970. Bumpers in turn was succeeded by Democrat David Pryor, who was replaced by Democrat William Clinton.

Regardless of whether the money is spent in the primary, the convention, or the general election, both figures need to be incorporated into the overall total spent in becoming governor. Even so, the knotty problem remains as to which vote to use in calculating the per vote expenditure. While in some cases the general election vote is a logical choice, the general election figure (in the solidly Democratic states, for example) misrepresents the amount spent per vote. As can be seen from the Alabama and Georgia examples, far more money is spent in the Democratic primary than in the general election. Thus, a better understanding of the cost is obtained if both the cost per vote in the general election and primary are shown separately. In a fifty-state comparison, this is frequently not feasible due to lack of separate data on the primary and the fact that in some states one party may use a convention for nominating candidates, as does the Republican party in Virginia. Thus, the best compromise seems to be to add the expenditures in both the primary and general election and to divide this total by the general election vote to get a total per vote figure. It should be understood, however, that Burns in Hawaii, Wallace in Alabama, and Carter in Georgia spent most of their money in the primary and not in the general election. Thus, the fairly substantial expenditures by Burns ($7.05), Wallace ($1.60), and Carter ($2.02) drop to a deceptive $2.00 for Burns, $0.15 for Wallace and $0.39 for Carter if the cost of the primary is not counted. Obviously, the use of the cost per vote in the general election alone does not present a true picture in all states. Consequently, the student of politics must know his state and look at the spending for the convention (if this can be obtained) or for both the primary and general election to get the most accurate picture of what is costs to become governor.

The general election for governor in New Jersey in 1977 was unique in that it was the first gubernatorial election in the United States financed partially with public funds. Under the Campaign Contributions and Expenditures Act, candidates who sought public financing were required to give a careful accounting of both their receipts and expenditures. These expenditures, therefore, provide a fairly accurate picture of the spending pattern in a modern gubernatorial election in our eighth largest state with a 1970 population of over 7 million inhabitants.

The New Jersey Election Law Enforcement Commission established an overall spending limitation of $1,518,576 for each candidate for the 1977 election. However, under the provisions of the act certain expenditures were not counted against the ceiling. These exempt expenditures included the candidates' travel; food and beverage fund-raising events; election night activities; and the amount of money a campaign staff spent to comply with the public financing statute. However, these exempt amounts did not constitute a major part of the candidates' expenditures. Brendan T. Byrne, the Democratic candidate, reported exempt expenditures of $161,471 while his Republican opponent Raymond H. Bateman's exempt expenses amounted to only $145,829. On the other hand, the expenditures that were subject to the overall limit amounted to about $1 million for each candidate. These expenditures are set out in Table 9.

If both the total expenditures exempt from limitation and those subject to limitation are added, it becomes apparent Byrne spent a total of $1,667,348 in the general election while Bateman spent $1,642,017. There is no official report on the expenditures in the primaries since these were not publicly financed in 1977. However, unofficial reports made by the candidates show that Byrne raised a total of $593,624 for the Democratic primary contest while Bateman raised a total of $964,466 for his race for the Republican nomination.

TABLE 9
THE EXPENDITURES OF MAJOR GUBERNATORIAL CANDIDATES IN THE NEW JERSEY GENERAL ELECTION OF 1977

Expenditures	Candidates	
	Byrne (D)	*Bateman (R)*
Administration including polls, office expenses, salaries, and telephones	$ 411,604	$ 486,468
Radio and television	805,096	661,217
Advertising production and consulting	180,000	96,021
Newspaper advertising	28,215	104,776
Billboards	———	66,973
Printing and mailing campaign literature	37,260	80,735
Expenditures by party committees	43,704	———
Total	$ 1,505,879	$ 1,496,188

SOURCE: Based on figures taken from *Public Financing in New Jersey: The 1977 General Election for Governor* (Trenton, N.J.: New Jersey Election Law Enforcement Commission, 1978), p. 43.

New Jersey is regarded by many observers as being two-party in its state politics, and the governorship has changed hands several times over the last twenty years. In spite of these shifts, more Democrats have served as governors than Republicans. Republican

Alfred E. Driscoll started off the 1950s with three successive victories, but then the Republicans' luck ran out. Driscoll was followed by two-term Democrat Robert E. Meyner, who was succeeded by two-term Democrat Richard J. Hughes. Then came a Republican interlude when William T. Cahill was elected in 1969. However, the short-lived Republican resurgence was terminated by the election of Democrat Brendan T. Byrne in 1973. Byrne thus was the incumbent in 1977; it is his reelection campaign in 1978 that is the subject of this discussion.

It was widely predicted that Byrne was vulnerable in 1977, but this apparently was not the case since he defeated Bateman in the general election with 55.7 percent of the vote. If we assume that New Jersey is, indeed, a two-party state and consider only the candidates' spending in the general election, a comparison of money spent to votes received shows that Byrne expended $1,667,348 and received 1,184,564 votes, spending $1.41 for each vote. Bateman, on the other hand, spent $1,642,017 but received only 888,880 votes for a cost of $1.85 per vote. Because of the spending limits established by statute, the New Jersey general election of 1977 was not one in which victory can be attributed to a candidate's superior financial resources. The campaigns of the two candidates, at least in the official reports, ran within $25,000 of each other with Byrne spending that amount more than Bateman. However, in a state in which the total expenditures in the general election alone were over $3 million, an expenditure of an additional $25,000 by one candidate cannot be considered of any real significance. The results in a campaign such as this in which the acceptance of public financing dictated almost equal spending must have been determined by factors other than money. Whether those factors were personalities, issues, party loyalty, the advantage of name recognition enjoyed by the incumbent, or some other response of the voters is a question whose answer is not found in an examination of the candidates' expenditures.

While $3 million is a large expenditure for a gubernatorial election even in a state with over 3.6 million registered voters, the New Jersey Election Law Enforcement Commission after a thorough study of the 1977 election recommended that "New Jersey should retain partial public financing of gubernatorial general elections and extend the concept to the primary elections for the governor beginning in 1981."[23] The commission also found that the candidates were able to raise substantial sums with a $600 ceiling on individual contributions. Governor Byrne received 48 percent of his total contributions in $600 amounts and Senator Bateman received 40 percent in that fashion. As was previously pointed out, the commission established a $1,518,576 limit on each one of the candidates in the campaign. Such a relatively generous limit allowed the candidates substantial sums of money for each of their campaigns. The limit is not the same for each election but is based on a sliding scale calculated by multiplying the number of votes cast in the immediately preceding general election by forty cents per vote. The recommendation of the committee was that this system be continued and that it also be applied to primaries as well, using a twenty cents per vote multiplier and a $600 per person contribution limit.

The matching funds provided by the state were quite substantial under the New Jersey plan in the 1977 general election with Byrne receiving $1,050,569 and Bateman $1,020,247 in public funds. The system is designed so that a candidate, to qualify for public funds, must first raise $40,000 in private funds. After he has met that minimum, the state then matches, on a two to one basis, the entire amount that is raised in contributions of no more than $600 per person until the private and state matching funds reach the allowed maximum. The commission has argued for the continuation of this system on the grounds that it " . . . is especially helpful to lesser known candidates or candidates who need to achieve name recognition."[24] As proof, the commission cited the fact that early in the 1977 campaign it had authorized the payment of $543,000 in public funds to Senator Bateman who was not so well known as Governor Byrne. As a result of Bateman's early spending "the polls indicated that from July to September there was a dramatic increase in the percentage of voters able to recognize his name."[25]

Based on the New Jersey experience in 1977, the commission felt that an overall limit on the total amount that a candidate and his supporters can spend is unnecessary and undesirable " . . . if the election process includes limits on contributions, loans and a candidate's own personal funds and a cap on the amount of public funds available to any candidate. . . . "[26] As was noted above, the cap which the commission recommended is a flexible one, based on twenty cents per vote for calculating the limit for public funds for the primary and forty cents per vote for the general election, using the number of voters who cast ballots in the most recent general election as the other factor in the equation. New Jersey elects its governors in odd years between presidential elections. Consequently, the turnout of voters in the presidential election just preceding the gubernatorial election would be the yardstick. Thus, the 1976 turnout in the presidential election was the basis for the 1977 calculations, the 1980 presidential election turnout was the basis for the 1981 gubernatorial election, and the number of voters for the 1985 gubernatorial election will be based on the 1984 presidential election.

The New Jersey plan has many strong points as it now stands. However, if it is expanded to include the primary, it should greatly reduce the impact of an individual's personal wealth. Under the present system of public financing in New Jersey, which covers the general election but not the primary, a candidate with substantial private funds has a definite advantage, although large personal expenditures do not always bring victory. The commission cites as an example one candidate who spent $135,000 of his own resources and an additional $148,000 contributed by his relatives in his unsuccessful primary effort. The $283,000 thus accumulated amounted to almost 50 percent of his total expenditures.[27]

In view of the emphasis in this section on the ever increasing cost of running for governor, it should be pointed out that it is not always necessary to spend vast sums of money to be elected even if one is a wealthy candidate. For example, in 1976 Congressman Pierre ("Pete") DuPont IV defeated the incumbent Governor Sherman Tribbitt with about 58 percent of the vote. DuPont, in order to overcome the millionaire image his family name evoked in Delaware, refused to accept contributions of more than $100 and limited his spending to a relatively modest $125,000. His campaign allegedly had financial troubles because of his contribution limit and had some difficulty in raising even the $125,000 that he did spend.[28] Unfortunately, Governor DuPont appears to be one of the last of a vanishing breed in the gubernatorial sweepstakes. Very substantial sums are now required to have a reasonable chance of winning the governorship in most states. Some better system seems necessary to assist the able but not personally wealthy candidate in his attempt to run for office. One answer is public financing, and New Jersey seems to have one of the best systems that has actually been placed in operation. The plan seems to have worked well in its initial trial in 1977 and, if extended to the primary, has much to recommend it for consideration by other states.

Generalizations about spending for television as opposed to radio or about the amount spent for the electronic media as opposed to print media are dangerous since the percentage spent for each varies from campaign to campaign. For example, in the Tennessee Democratic primary in 1974, the winning candidate's expenditures were 46 percent for television, 31 percent for billboards, 19 percent for print advertising, and 5 percent for the cost of the public relations firm directing his campaign. In another state in the same year, the breakdown was quite different in that only 22 percent of the candidate's budget was earmarked for television. In yet another campaign, only 31 percent of campaign funds were designated for radio and television, but 32 percent was spent on the print media.

One problem in discussing detailed expenditures by category is that, even in states in which the candidates are required to report their expenditures, the amount spent for radio and television may be lumped together. The same item frequently includes expenses for advertising agencies, and is not always clearly defined since it may or may not include the amount paid to political consultants. Thus, it is difficult to get a firm grasp of each type of media spending.

Additional examples of campaign expenditures are helpful but not conclusive in determining the effectiveness of media spending. For instance, in the 1973 gubernatorial race in Virginia, the winner spent 41 percent of his budget on television, radio, and advertising agency expenses. The loser, however, spent only 29 percent of his total funds on the electronic media and advertising agency assistance. Larry Sabato in analyzing this election notes that Mills E. Goodwin, the winning Republican candidate, spent almost $164,000 more on media advertising than his opponent, Independent Henry Howell. Sabato concludes that a good portion of this $164,000 was concentrated on a media blitz during the final two weeks of the campaign. "Howell, it would appear from the spending reports, used too much too early, and was not financially able to counter the effective media campaign of his opponent in the home stretch."[29]

In the 1979 gubernatorial campaign in Kentucky, Democratic candidate John Y. Brown is reported to have spent $300,000 on television and radio. His campaign was wrapped up with a very expensive, statewide, ten-minute television spot pulling out all the stops including a musical background featuring "My Old Kentucky Home" played on the guitar.

In New Jersey in 1977, the winning candidate reported spending 48.3 percent on radio and television while the loser spent only 40.3 percent on the electronic media. As was previously noted, the campaign was partially financed with public funds and had a legal spending limit. Thus, the difference was particularly significant and may have influenced the course of the campaign. Each candidate made a deliberate choice as to where he would spend his legally limited funds. For instance, the winner spent only 1.7 percent of his budget on newspaper advertising while the loser spent 6.4 percent of his funds on this type of advertising. The Republican challenger also spent 4.1 percent on billboards while his opponent spent none.

In the Missouri campaign in 1976, the winning candidate is reported to have spent about two-thirds of his total campaign chest on television. On the other hand, the loser spent only about one-half of his funds on that medium.[30] In this race the actual dollars spent were almost even, but the winner spent a larger percentage of his total budget on television than did the loser. As suggested earlier, the key factor in this television campaign apparently was that the winner spent most heavily in the closing days of the general election campaign.

The six major candidates in the 1979 Louisiana nonpartisan primary spent between 41 percent and 63 percent of their budgets on the media including radio, television, and newspaper production and advertising. The two winning candidates in the primary, David Treen (Republican) and Louis Lambert (Democrat), spent 43 percent and 42 percent respectively on the media for the primary and general election. The dollar outlay was staggering: Treen's media bill totaled $2.6 million and Lambert's, about $2 million. In addition, Treen spent another $400,000 on professional services, and

Lambert spent $934,000. These services included campaign strategists, polling, telephone banks, accounting, legal services, and computer work.[31]

On the average in the races cited above, about 38 percent of total expenditures were devoted to the electronic media. However, because of the limited sample and the ambiguity found in much of the expenditure reports, it is doubtful that this average is statistically valid. Nevertheless, the average does tend to agree with the information gained in interviews from what should probably be called "sometimes reliable sources." These informants suggested that an expenditure, on an average, of 40 percent for the electronic media would be about right. However, some pointed out campaigns in which they estimated that over 50 percent of the campaign funds went to television alone. Others stressed the continuing importance of organization and "old-fashioned" campaigning, and maintained that in their states a 25 percent expenditure for television and radio would be adequate.

The most widely accepted conclusion among those interviewed on the role of the electronic media in gubernatorial campaigning was that the addition of radio and television, particularly television, has increased the cost of campaigning sharply. Especially in California and New York those interviewed cited the almost astronomical sums it takes to buy television time in the major viewing areas of those states with their tremendous market potential. However, even in a medium-size state like Tennessee, which ranked seventeenth in population with 3,924,000 persons in 1970, the rates for television ads increased 300 percent between 1972 and 1979, and one thirty-second spot ad in 1979 in a big television market like Memphis or Nashville would have cost the candidate $750. Of course, inflation has increased all campaign costs, but none have risen as sharply as television. For example in the same six-year period cited above, radio rates increased by only 65 percent. Printing costs for posters and handbills went up 45 percent, and the cost of placing a political ad in a newspaper increased 48 percent. Even the cost of the lowly campaign button jumped from nine cents in 1972 to thirteen cents in 1979.[32]

Another example of the rising costs of any campaign is the increase in the cost of direct mail advertising, which is still used extensively in some states. This form of political advertising is probably the most costly in terms of its coverage and effect. Normally such mailing uses bulk rate, but even so it involves a substantial cost for postage not counting the time and money involved in preparing a brochure or letter for mailing. To place a piece of campaign literature in the hands of all potential voters over eighteen years old in California would cost $1,246,560 in postage alone; in New York the same mailing would cost $1,073,604, and in Illinois, $642,936. In the smaller states the cost would be much more modest: in Nevada, $33,768, and in Vermont, only $26,880. Of course, it is not likely that any candidate would engage in such indiscriminate mailing since the first rule in a direct mail campaign is to mail only to a carefully selected list of voters who might be expected to regard the candidate in a favorable light. However, if it is assumed that the campaign coordinator has a carefully selected list of only 50,000 names, it would still cost $4,200 to mail a modest folded brochure. If the same individuals are contacted by mail more than once, and they generally are in a mail campaign, the outlay can be substantial. If the campaign director should decide to use first-class mail on the theory that a first-class letter is more likely to be read, it would cost $10,000 for one-shot coverage of 50,000 potential voters.

It is easy to spend considerable sums of money in a gubernatorial race, and it is difficult to be elected without considerable financial backing. The cost of campaigning is one of the unsolved dilemmas of the American democratic system. However, federal funding of presidential races and the newer moves toward state funding of gubernatorial races are steps in the right direction.

Notes

1. Coleman B. Ransone, Jr., *The Office of Governor in the United States* (University, Ala.: University of Alabama Press, 1956), p. 97.

2. The idea was suggested to Finch by his political consultant, Bill Jones, who operates Viewpoint, a public relations and political consulting firm in Montgomery, Alabama. In addition to the Finch campaign, Viewpoint has handled a number of successful gubernatorial and other campaigns in the South. Letter to the author from Bill Jones, March 30, 1980.

3. Jimmy Carter, *Why Not the Best?* (Nashville, Tenn.: Broadman Press, 1976), p. 114.

4. Robert Pack, *Jerry Brown: The Philosopher-Prince* (New York: Stein and Day, 1978), p. xiii.

5. Tommy Stevenson, "He's a Politician without the Election," *Tuscaloosa* (Ala.) *News,* 27 August 1978, sec. D, p. 3.

6. *Tuscaloosa* (Ala.) *News,* 27 August 1978, sec. D, p. 3.

7. Buckley v. Valeo, 424 U.S. 1 (1976).

8. Data furnished by Don Seigelman, Secretary of State, State of Alabama.

9. Reports on file with the state librarian, Nashville, Tennessee.

10. Richard W. Hall-Sizemore, "Money in Politics: Financing the 1977 Statewide Elections in Virginia," *University of Virginia Newsletter* 56 (August 1980), p. 46.

11. *PAR Analysis: The Great Louisiana Campaign Spendathon,* Public Affairs Research Council of Louisiana Pamphlet no. 243 (March 1980), pp. 2–7.

12. See Table 4 and the accompanying discussion in chapter 1 for an explanation of these party categories.

13. "Survey on State Campaign Finance," *Comparative State Politics Newsletter* [University of Kentucky] 1 (January 1980): 22–23.

14. Tony Quinn, "Political Action Committees—The New Campaign Bankrollers," *California Journal,* March 1979, p. 37.

15. *The Annual Statistical Report of Expenditures Made in Connection with the 1976 Elections,* prepared by James C. Kirkpatrick, secretary of state, Missouri, 12 May 1977, pp. 46–48, 314–15.

16. *Kansas City* (Mo.) *Times,* 2 December 1976, p. 7.

17. Robert J. Gwyn, "The Power of the Press: Broadcast Media," *Popular Government* [University of North Carolina] 44 (Fall 1978): 6.

18. Tom Coffman, *Catch a Wave: A Case Study of Hawaii's New Politics* (Honolulu: University Press of Hawaii, 1973), p. 201.

19. Stuart Gerry Brown, foreword to Coffman, *Catch a Wave,* pp. x–xi.

20. Hickel resigned to become the United States Secretary of the Interior and was replaced by Lieutenant Governor Keith H. Miller for one year, 1969–70.

21. The figures on campaign expenditures are taken from Larry Sabato, *Goodbye to Good-time Charlie: The American Governor Transformed, 1950-1975* (Lexington, Mass.: D.C. Heath, 1978), pp. 157–59, except for the figures on Hawaii which are from Coffman, *Catch a Wave,* p. 201. The cost per vote does not agree with Sabato's calculations which were based only on the amount spent in the general election. My calculations are based on spending in both the primary and general election.

22. The Hawaii campaign figures were supplied by Common Cause, Hawaii. The Alaska figures are from Rhodes Cook and Stacy West, "1978 Gubernatorial Contests: Incumbent Winners Hold Money Advantage," *Congressional Quarterly Weekly Report,* 25 August 1979, pp. 1755–56.

23. New Jersey Election Law Enforcement Commission, *Public Financing in New Jersey: The 1977 General Election for Governor* (Trenton, N.J., 1978), p. 30.

24. Ibid., p. 32.

25. Ibid., p. 32.

26. Ibid., p. 34.

27. Ibid., p. 37.

28. *Time,* 15 November 1976, p. 55.

29. Larry Sabato, *Aftermath of "Armageddon": An Analysis of the 1973 Virginia Gubernatorial Election* (Charlottesville, Va.: Institute of Government, University of Virginia, 1975), p. 85.

30. *Kansas City* (Mo.) *Times,* 2 December 1976, p. 7.

31. *The Great Louisiana Campaign Spendathon,* p. 5.

32. *Washington Post,* 9 October 1979, sec. A, p. 4.

3

THE CHARACTER OF THE
EXECUTIVE FUNCTION

As might be expected, in dealing with fifty states, each with a different history, a different cultural heritage, and sometimes with considerable differences in forms of government, we find distinct variations from state to state in the governor's functions. These functions also tend to change over time. Nevertheless, it is the thesis of this chapter that out of these variations emerges a hard core of gubernatorial powers and duties which are sufficiently similar in all states to warrant the formulation of an "executive function" at the state level. Briefly stated, this concept of executive function is based on the fact that the modern American governor is primarily concerned with three broad areas of operations—policy formation, public relations, and management. Of these, policy formation is the most important but public relations appears to be the most time-consuming. Management tends to fall in second place in terms of importance and time devoted to it by the governor.

It should be emphasized at the outset of the discussion that, although this definition of the governor's functions has considerable practical validity, it can by no means be applied as a formula that automatically defines the executive function in a given state under a given governor. The functions that are actually performed by the governor of a particular state depend on several factors, of which the more important are the gubernatorial powers and duties established by the state constitution, the attitude of the legislature on the question of the proper scope of gubernatorial power, the power or lack of power stemming from the governor's position in his party, and the powers and limitations attached to the office as a result of custom and tradition. The functions and duties on which a governor chooses to spend his time will vary from governor to governor even in the same state, depending on the incumbent's concept of the governorship.

Conditioning Factors

The functions performed by the modern American governor are conditioned by many rather complex factors. One of these is the fact that the constitutional basis for the governor's powers is more limited in some states than in others. The statutes enacted by the legislature over the years that either increase or limit his constitutional powers is another important consideration. The governor's position in his party is also a factor which tends either to strengthen or weaken his power in relation to his legislative and management duties. Equally important, however, are the customs and traditions of the state which, over a long period of time, seem to set the tone of state government. In some states the cumulative effects of custom and tradition tend to make the governor more powerful than he would appear to be from an examination of the statutes, while in others they seem to limit the governor's powers, although he may be equally strong in terms of his constitutional powers. Added to these considerations is the view of the governor's proper role held by successive incumbents of the office. While this view tends to be shaped by the customs and traditions of the state and hence tends to be similar in successive governors of the same state, the governor's idea of his proper function is also significant. This is particularly true in determining which aspect of the governor's duties shall receive the major emphasis. Granted that he must perform certain functions under the statutes, the governor still has considerable leeway in determining which functions will receive the most emphasis, and this emphasis is important in shaping operations.

A good illustration of this point was the view held by Francis Sargent, the governor of Massachusetts from 1969 to 1975. According to Martha Weinberg, Governor Sargent did not enjoy his management functions and " . . . therefore did not accord it a favored position among his duties."[1] Sargent also relinquished the governor's normal role as legislative leader, apparently for two reasons. In the first place, Sargent was a Republican and the legislature overwhelmingly Democratic during his six years in office. Thus, he felt that he had a built-in partisan opposition to his program. Second, although he was a Republican, the Republican minority in the legislature had no strong personal loyalty to him as party leader. Therefore, what normally would have been a legislative bloc upon which he could build was denied him. He concluded that he had little chance of working with the legislature in such a way that he could give the public appearance of forceful leadership. Consequently, his " . . . strategy was often to avoid the costs of dealing with the General Court and to portray himself and his policies as the 'victims' of a partisan and parochial legislature."[2]

What Governor Sargent liked to do was to carry out the ceremonial functions of the governorship, and he spent more than half of his time on these functions, including a large number of public appearances. These appearances, of course, were tied in with his own campaigning both for reelection and to build a base of support for his policies independent of the formal party structure. While Governor Sargent had to devote some time to "legislative leadership" and to "management," his personality and personal preferences led him to spend most of his time on the "public relations" function of the governor. While this emphasis was partly due to his political situation, it would appear that the emphasis was a matter of choice. The difference in gubernatorial style is certainly one of the crucial factors affecting the governor's exercise of his functions.

While some of this change in emphasis from governor to governor may be due to political considerations, a good deal of it can be attributed to nothing more complex than what a governor likes to do. Some governors, although not many, are administratively minded; most governors, with a few exceptions, are "policy" minded. All governors must spend some time on "public relations" but some, like Governor Sargent, especially enjoy this role. Generally, these governors are extremely good at the person-to-person approach that makes them effective not only at "ceremonial" duties but also at politics.

Governor Sargent's view of his role—different from that of his predecessors—points up the fact that a governor's concept of the gubernatorial function may have as much to do with shaping that function in a particular state as do the constitutional and statutory powers. A listing of the legal powers of the governor, therefore, is only a beginning in understanding those powers and explains little of their importance as opposed to the impact of culture, tradition, politics, and the governor's own view of his functions. It is for this reason that the following analysis of the governor's functions is based on what a governor actually does rather than on the more traditional assessment of his legal authority and responsibilities. This analysis is the basis for the formulation of the governor's functions found in this chapter.

Demands on the Governor's Time

One of the least understood facets of the governorship is what a typical governor actually does with his time. The many requests from citizen groups for the governor to speak at local meetings of various kinds, the constant stream of visitors who flood the governor's office, and the innumerable letters containing every conceivable request, all indicate that the average citizen apparently thinks that the governor is an official who not only has unlimited time for the problems of individual citizens but also has equally unlimited power to solve them. It seems inconceivable that the governor does not have time to settle a boundary dispute between two neighbors or does not have the power to get "my boy" out of a federal prison. This concept of gubernatorial infallibility has been subtly encouraged by those governors who have adopted an "open-door" policy under which one day a week is set aside for citizens of the state to see the governor. This is undoubtedly in accord with the democratic tradition in this country and with local tradition in many states. However, such a policy is not without severe limitations, not the least of which is the fact that if the governor spends even a day a week on individual interviews, he has a day less to attend to other facets of state business. Time is of the essence to the governor who is a busy individual and follows a daily schedule that leaves him little personal life.

The time devoted to various activities varies from state to state depending on the population of the state and the personality of a particular governor. In the smaller states the office tends to be more personal. The governor has a small staff and does more business through personal interviews and telephone calls and less through his staff and correspondence. In the larger states his schedule is more formalized, and his office is larger and more highly organized. He spends less time seeing people since much of this work is delegated to members of his staff.

The governor's personality and work habits also have a marked effect on his schedule. For example, some governors do little correspondence at their office and prefer to take care of this chore at home after office hours. On the other hand, some governors like to begin the day by clearing up a major part of their correspondence. Others begin the day with a press conference or with conferences with their department heads. In some states the governor handles a great deal of business by telephone, while in others more business is handled through personal interviews and correspondence.

It should be understood also that the governor is not in his office every day. As a general rule, he is out of the office at least one day a week because he spends considerable time traveling throughout the state to deliver speeches, attend various meetings, and participate in other activities away from the capitol.

An analysis of the governor's day in the 1950s revealed that he devoted approximately four and one-half hours a day to conferences and interviews exclusive of press conferences. This figure seems, at first glance, to be rather startling but it is supported by several actual analyses of the governor's work load. For example, a "desk audit" of the governor of Arkansas over a four-day period revealed that the governor received one hundred callers in this period, or an average of twenty-five persons a day. If each of these visitors spent only ten minutes with the governor, these interviews would occupy over four hours of his time. However, interviews usually cannot be dispensed with so expeditiously and telephone calls and interruptions greatly increased the time that they took.[3]

A detailed study of the activities of the governor of New Hampshire over a three-week period in 1950 revealed that the governor of that state spent about three and one-half hours a day on interviews and conferences.[4] An average of several one- or two-day samples which I obtained during my first field trips in the early 1950s and the estimates of the governor's executive secretaries in the states covered during that period indicate that the average American governor saw from ten to twenty-five persons a day. The period during which the state legislature was in session was the busiest time of the year in regard to conferences. When the legislature was not in session, the governor probably saw an average of fifteen persons a day, but when the legislature was in session the total was closer to twenty-five.

A comparison of the daily schedules of governors in the 1950s with those of governors in the 1970s reveals that the earlier governors spent more time on formal press conferences than do their modern counterparts. In the fifties the average governor held two half-hour press conferences a day, although frequently the conferences did not last for the entire period scheduled. In some of the smaller states, there were no formally scheduled conferences. For example, in Vermont only two correspondents regularly covered the capitol beat in the early 1950s. Under these circumstances there was no need for two formal press conferences a day. When the governor had an item of interest to the press, he called in the press representatives for a conference or gave them the information when they dropped into the office informally to check up on latest developments. As a result of these informal arrangements, the governor of Vermont spent only about twenty minutes a day on interviews with the press. In South Dakota, the governor found it necessary to have only one press conference each morning and spent only about thirty minutes a day on this aspect of his duties.

The schedule for handling press relations depends primarily on two factors, the number of correspondents covering the capitol beat and the presence or absence of both morning and afternoon papers. If there are a large number of correspondents at the capitol, it is a more economical use of the governor's time to call in these representatives as a group for a press conference. If there are only one or two press representatives at the capitol, press relations can be handled more informally, and the governor can afford to see the representatives of the press individually on matters that are considered newsworthy.

In several small states in the 1950s, however, the governor had two press conferences a day or was available for two interviews at different times because the capitol beat was covered by representatives of both a morning and an evening paper. Since these papers had different deadlines, holding only one press conference a day would have given the advantage to the evening paper if it had been held in the early morning or to the morning paper if it had been held in the afternoon. The timing of important announcements by the governor is a matter for calculation, and he must try to release an equal amount of important news at each press conference or at least alternately at the morning and afternoon sessions throughout the week.

Typically, therefore, in the 1950s two press conferences a day were used by most governors because there was ordinarily coverage by both morning and evening newspapers. It might seem that these conferences could be handled by the governor's press secretary or executive secretary, with the governor appearing in person only on very important occasions. In some instances this was done, but the general rule was that the governor appeared personally at the conference. In the 1950s the press looked with suspicion on press releases or secondhand information, and such was their power of persuasion in that era that they generally carried the day in demanding a personal appearance. This was not true in New York, however, where Governor Thomas E. Dewey (1942–1955) did not have regularly scheduled press conferences. Apparently this was the only state in the 1950s in which the governor did not comply with the demand of the press for the governor's personal attendance at regularly scheduled press conferences or availability for frequent interviews as the sine qua non for adequate coverage of the capitol beat.

The situation in the 1970s in relation to the press is quite different from that in the 1950s because of the growing importance of television during the last thirty years. What could be legitimately called press relations in the 1950s has now become media relations and generally involves not only the press but radio and television reporters as well. Television, especially, has changed the format and timing of the governor's "press" conferences. They now have become media events, and tend to be fewer in number and more formalized in style in most states than they were in the 1950s.

A third duty of the governor in the fifties as revealed by his daily timetable was answering correspondence, telegrams, and telephone calls. The amount of time devoted by the governor to this aspect of his daily routine varied considerably from state to state and appears to have been determined more by the governor's own view of the amount of time which should be devoted to this function than by the volume of correspondence, although the latter, of course, had some effect. Even in the 1950s the governor did not read or answer all his mail personally, and this is certainly the case with the governor in the seventies. In most offices in the 1970s an effective system of tabulating and sorting mail has been established, with all mail being logged in and out of the office and a record kept of the action taken on each piece of mail. The mail is sorted initially by a member of the governor's staff who uses previously agreed upon guidelines for routing the mail. Some of it is sent to the department most directly involved, and some is sent to one of the governor's assistants for reply.

In smaller states the executive secretary or another trusted staff member still reads all incoming mail and screens it so that out of one hundred or so letters a day the governor will actually see only a dozen. Some governors, however, like to read a cross section of the incoming mail to get a feel for the public pulse. These governors, consequently, spend more of their time in reading and answering correspondence.

Estimates on the amount of time which the governor spent on correspondence in the 1950s ranged from ninety minutes to three hours a day, with the average time being about two hours. In the 1970s the volume of mail has increased with the average governor's office receiving at least 500 pieces of mail a day and perhaps from 200 to 250 telephone calls. However, it does not appear that the amount of time devoted by the governor to his mail also has increased.[5]

The amount of time a governor devotes to his mail is a personal decision. For example, one governor who was interviewed said that he regarded correspondence as his homework and that it took a large proportion of his free time. His wife confirmed this statement indirectly by saying that the governor worked until twelve or one o'clock each night and that in her opinion the executive mansion was too close to the capitol.

The handling of correspondence was an important problem in the governor's offices in the 1950s and still remains a significant problem in the 1970s in spite of the fact that the mechanics of gubernatorial mail handling has undoubtedly improved. The problem is as significant in the seventies as it was in the fifties because an unanswered letter or a bungled reply creates poor public relations for the governor. Consequently, the contemporary governor, as did his counterpart thirty years ago, still tries to ensure that his mail is handled as accurately and as rapidly as possible.

In addition to correspondence, the governor makes and receives a large number of phone calls each day, most of which are to or from distant points in the state or throughout the United States. These phone calls are frequently almost as time-consuming as correspondence. The relative amount of time spent on phone calls and correspondence varies considerably from state to state and seems to depend to a considerable degree on the geographical configuration of the state and on the density of population. For example, in those northeastern states which are compact and rather densely populated, the governor gets about two letters for every phone call. On the other hand, in those southwestern states which are characterized by a large area and a small population, much of the governor's business is handled by long distance telephone calls. Several governors in the Southwest suggested that the long distances involved made it relatively difficult for citizens to come to the office with their problems and that they used the telephone as a substitute for a personal visit. In these states the ratio of phone calls to letters is approximately two to one.

While no typical pattern emerges from these figures, it appears that a considerable amount of the business of the governor's office is conducted by telephone, with the use of the telephone being greater relative to written communications in the southwestern states. In the rest of the nation, the volume of correspondence equals or exceeds incoming and outgoing telephone calls.

An analysis of the governor's day in the 1950s revealed that he was occupied principally with conferences with department heads, legislators, the press, and the general public and with the handling of correspondence and telephone calls. In addition, he had a great many functions after hours, which one governor termed his extracurricular activities. These functions, such as speeches, banquets, and radio and television appearances, were very time-consuming;

and, together with press conferences and interviews, they formed the core of the governor's public relations activities.

One of the most complete analyses of a governor's schedule in the late 1940s and early 1950s was a study based on the daily engagement book kept by the secretary to Governor Sherman Adams of New Hampshire. The study covered three weeks, selected at random, beginning on 4 April, 23 May, and 12 December 1949. Since the data on which the study is based is for 1949, it is not completely accurate to use it as an example of the governor's functions in the 1950s. However, Governor Adams's first term from 1949 to 1950 took him into the fifties and his second term from 1951 to 1953 carried him still further into that era. Furthermore, when I interviewed the governor during his second term, it did not appear that his functions had changed substantially from those reported in the analysis. Consequently, it is probably typical of Governor Adams's second term as well. Of course, no one governor is ever representative of a particular period of time or of all the states. Governor Adams was the governor of a small New England state that was then heavily Republican, had one of the largest legislatures in the United States in spite of its small population, and had a number of ethnic, political, and economic features to differentiate it from many other states. Consequently, this analysis should be taken simply as an illustration of the way one governor spent his time in the 1950s. It is significant to know that the periods covered by the analysis included two weeks in which the legislature was in session and one week after the legislature had adjourned. Thus we get a better balanced picture of the governor's day in that the work of Governor Adams was not skewed greatly by the increased involvement with the legislature during the two weeks in which it was in session.

This analysis of the governor's work week shows that Governor Adams worked sixty-eight, sixty-seven, and fifty-six hours respectively during these three weeks. The governor's average work week therefore would be approximately sixty-three and one-half hours which would be broken down as shown in Table 10.

Table 10 and the two tables which follow it reflect the interests of the persons making the various studies. The study summarized in Table 10 was made by a reorganization commission for New Hampshire. Apparently, they were interested primarily in how

TABLE 10
AN ANALYSIS OF THE WEEKLY SCHEDULE OF THE GOVERNOR OF NEW HAMPSHIRE, 1949

Activity	Hours		Percentage
Correspondence	9 2/3		15.2
Phone calls	3 1/2		5.5
Interviews	20		31.5
With members of the legislature		5	7.9
With department heads and officers		4 1/3	6.8
With citizens		4	6.3
With job seekers		1 1/3	2.1
With the press		1	1.6
On industrial development		1	1.6
With party leaders		1	1.6
On state reorganization		1	1.6
On employee reclassification study		2/3	1.0
On miscellaneous matters		2/3	1.0
Meetings	7 1/3		11.5
Of governor's council		4	6.3
With state boards and commissions		2	3.1
On political matters		1 1/3	2.1
Preparing and giving speeches	3 1/2		5.5
Travel	10 1/2		16.5
Dignitary matters (such affairs as christening USS *Pickerel,* bill-signing ceremonies, meeting groups of schoolchildren, acting as honored guest at various meetings)	9		14.2
Total	63 1/2		99.9

SOURCE: Coleman B. Ransone, Jr., *The Office of Governor in the United States* (University Ala.: University of Alabama Press, 1956), p. 137.
NOTE: Percentages do not add up to 100 due to rounding.

many hours the governor worked and what he did in a rather literal sense. For example, we know from the table that the governor spent five hours in conferences with members of the legislature. However, the table gives us no clue as to what was discussed in these sessions. In other words, there is very little content analysis in this particular study.

In contrast, the study which is summarized in Table 11 has much more content analysis because it was done by Ronald D. Michaelson who was the governor's assistant. Among other things, Michaelson was interested in comparing the governor's functions in Illinois in 1971 with those found in my earlier study of *The Office of Governor in the United States* made in 1956. While Michaelson accepted two of the categories—public relations and management—used in that study, he felt that the third category of policy formation was too broad and therefore he dissected it. This dissection took place in additional tables that broke down such broad items as legislative relations and political leadership into their component parts and through the commentary accompanying these tables.

TABLE 11
AN ANALYSIS OF A MONTHLY SCHEDULE OF THE GOVERNOR OF ILLINOIS, JUNE 1971

Category	Hours	Percentage of Total Scheduled Time
Public relations	67	27
Management of state government	48	19
Personal (invitations to private functions)	44	18
Legislative relations	39	16
Political leadership	27	11
Intra-office responsibilities	14	6
Out-of-state travel	12	5
Total	251	102

SOURCE: Adapted from Ronald D. Michaelson, "An Analysis of the Chief Executive: How the Governor Uses His Time," *State Government* 45 (Summer 1972): 155.
NOTE: The percentages do not add up to 100 due to rounding.

The most comprehensive presentation of the way the governors spent their time in the seventies was provided by a study of the National Governors' Association made in 1976. This study is particularly interesting in that it has the estimate of the governor's scheduling secretary as to how much time the governor spent on various functions and also has a fairly representative sample of sixteen governors who indicated how they had spent their time (see Table 12). Naturally, the table reflects the interest of the persons preparing the study. As will be noted, it does not divide the governor's functions into the three categories which I used in 1956 nor does it use the categories found in the Michaelson study. Rather it divides the functions of the governor into those categories which seemed appropriate to the scholars making the survey for the National Governors' Association.

TABLE 12
HOW GOVERNORS SPEND THEIR TIME
(in percentage of total work time)

Activity	Schedulers' Estimates	Governors' Estimates
Managing state government	29	27
Working with the legislature	16	18
Meeting the general public	14	—
Ceremonial functions	14	13
Working with the press and media	9	7
Working with the federal government	7	7
Working with local governments	7	7
Political activities	6	8
Recruiting and appointing	6	8
Miscellaneous activities	16	9

SOURCE: Center for Policy Research, *Governing the American States: A Handbook for New Governors* (Washington, D.C.: National Governors' Association, 1978), p. 277.

NOTE: Percentages in the first column (schedulers' estimates) are based on responses from those handling the governor's schedule in forty states; percentages in the second column (governors' estimates) are based on responses from governors of sixteen states. Totals do not add up to 100 percent, but are averages of the respondents' estimates of the portion of a governor's time devoted to a particular activity.

This study probably is a more accurate reflection of a governor's schedules than either Michaelson's single state study or my summary of twenty-five states made in 1956 because of its broader coverage. The first column covers some forty states, although these figures actually are only estimates. In addition, in the second column the table also covers the estimates of sixteen governors. The categories are really not very far apart, except for one item—"meeting the general public"—for which the governors allotted no time for reasons not explained in the study. Otherwise, the small percentage changes among items makes no essential difference in the concept of what the governor does. It would appear from looking at this table that managing the state government (which can either be 29 or 27 percent, depending on the choice of columns) would be the principal function of the governor. However, if in the first column "meeting the general public" (14 percent), "ceremonial functions" (14 percent), and "working with the press and media" (9 percent) are combined, this total of 37 percent for public relations makes it the most time-consuming function of the governor. This relationship between public relations and management is exactly what I found in 1956 so that the time devoted to this function does not seem to have changed appreciably over the twenty-year period.

The second major function of the governor in terms of time devoted to it then becomes the management of state government. It definitely is my impression that the governors in the 1950s were not putting 27 to 29 percent of their time into the management of state government. Consequently, either of these figures would represent a shift in the 1970s in the direction of a greater emphasis on management.

It should also be pointed out that apparently no time was devoted to policy formation as such. However, it seems probable that a good deal of the activity under such headings as "working with the federal government" (7 percent), "working with local governments" (7 percent), and certainly at least part of "political activities" (6 percent) must have had something to do with policy formation. I would also be inclined to put all of "working with the legislature" at 16 percent under this heading because it is through the legislature that the governor generally makes principal policy changes.

It is extremely difficult to compare the data that I collected in 1956 to Michaelson's in 1971 and to compare both of these with the data from the National Governors' Association study in 1976. However, it should be noted that the governor of Illinois spent only 19 percent of his time on the management of state government according to Michaelson, a figure at variance with the 29 percent that the governors' schedulers estimated that the governors spent on management in the National Governors' Association table. The analysis given in the text of the study by the National Governors' Association does not give a detailed breakdown of the governor's management function. However, the study does state that most of the time in that category "is devoted to meetings in the governor's office with agency heads, board or commission members, and staff members. A small portion of it is spent in state offices, institutions and other state facilities."[6]

Another approach in determining how a governor uses his time is to ask how the governors would respond to typical scheduling requests. The results of this survey are shown in the next table, which provides some clues as to the kinds of activities that a governor finds important. For example, a state fair opening is obviously of considerable importance since 68 percent of the governors replying to this particular item indicated that they would accept an invitation to open the state fair. Also of considerable importance are requests by legislators to see the governor. Note that a request by even a freshman legislator to see the governor with no subject specified generally would be granted by 82 percent of the governors. Furthermore, a senior legislator, such as a committee chairman, would generally be given an appointment by 92 percent of the governors, while 90 percent generally would see the leader of the opposition. It would also appear that labor is high on the list because the annual meeting of the American Federation of Labor–Congress of Industrial Organizations (AFL-CIO) statewide organization would have received a positive reply from 79 percent of the governors.

If we add the "generally" and "sometimes" columns together, we get a higher total but it seems a better comparison to use only those governors who would "generally" respond favorably. As can be seen by their response patterns (see Table 13), politics certainly is as significant as any other factor in the governor's decision as to whom he will see.

TABLE 13
GOVERNORS' RESPONSES TO TYPICAL SCHEDULING REQUESTS

Event or Request	Percentage of Governors Who Would Accede to Request		
	Generally	*Sometimes*	*Rarely*
Request by senior legislator (e.g., committee chairman) to see governor with no subject specified	92	5	3
Request by legislative leader of opposition party to see governor with no subject specified	90	5	5
Request by freshman legislator to see governor with no subject specified	82	10	8
Address annual AFL-CIO statewide meeting	79	18	3
State fair opening	68	13	19
Request by legislator for meeting with group of constituents visiting state capitol with no special business to conduct	68	26	5
Address annual meeting of state chamber of commerce	58	39	3
Highway ribbon cutting	26	47	26
Address annual meeting of association of homebuilders	26	67	8
Head of small teachers organization wishing to talk to governor about increased school aid	21	51	28
Head of school administrators association (statewide) wishing to talk to governor about increased school aid	21	51	28

Table 13 — Continued

Event or Request	Percentage of Governors Who Would Accede to Request		
	Generally	*Sometimes*	*Rarely*
100th anniversary ceremonies for community of 5,000 people	18	42	39
County fair opening	17	39	44
Group wanting to complain about a department head	14	39	47
Individual citizen with no prior contact with governor and no organization affiliation wishing to talk to governor about abortion	5	18	77

SOURCE: Based on data taken from Center for Policy Research, *Governing American States: A Handbook for New Governors* (Washington, D.C.: National Governors' Association, 1978), p. 278.

NOTE: Responses do not always total 100 percent due to rounding.

While the material which has been presented in this section shows considerable state-to-state variation and some variation over time, it also shows that the governors have many common duties and functions in their daily routines. Perhaps the most significant point is the amount of time which the governor spends on correspondence, telephone calls, interviews, travel, and speech making. While all of these may be concerned with either policy or management, they may also be classified partly as public relations. Most of the governor's correspondence and telephone calls as well as the majority of his interviews are concerned with problems that are presented by the state's citizens rather than by party leaders, legislators, or department heads. These contacts with the citizens of the state together with the governor's public speeches, his radio and television appearances, and his attendance either as a speaker or as an honored guest at numerous banquets, cornerstone laying ceremonies, state fairs, and rodeos fall in the general category of public relations. This aspect of the governor's functions emerges as the most time-consuming if not the most important of his duties on the basis of the evidence presented in this section. It is interesting to compare the findings of this section with the views of the governor's functions as seen by the governors themselves in the following section. Such a comparison reveals that while the governors do not give public relations as high a ranking as the time actually spent on it would indicate, it nevertheless is a segment of their duties of which most governors are aware and on which they place considerable weight.

The Governors' Views of the Executive Function

Another approach in determining the gubernatorial function is to examine statements of the governors' duties and responsibilities as formulated by the governors themselves. These statements generally are taken from interviews with the governors or from articles and speeches by the governors. The governors' own evaluation of their duties and responsibilities tends to be in terms of their relative importance rather than in terms of the time spent on them, although several of the statements combine both approaches. The time a governor spends on a particular function is one indication of its importance, although it is not an infallible guide since for statutory or other reasons the governor may be forced to spend considerable time on a function that he personally regards as unimportant.

Apparently, most governors are not given to philosophizing about the nature of the office, for speeches or articles in which a governor describes his functions are relatively rare. However, several of the governors have been moved to describe their version of the functions of the state's chief executive in fairly complete form, and several others have made statements pointing to the importance of certain functions of the office. All of the governors interviewed were asked to comment on important aspects of the governorship, and most of them had quite definite views. The initial statement of their functions given by most governors tended to be a fairly standard list of their legal duties, such as the appointment of certain state officers, recommending bills to the legislature, and the preparation of the budget. However, the more detailed questioning during the interviews generally revealed the governor's view of the relative importance of his functions.

The quotations from the governors are arranged so that the first group of comments comes from governors serving in the late 1940s and 1950s, and the second group is from governors serving in the 1960s and 1970s. While the first group of statements is fairly representative of the governors in the fifties and the second group of the seventies, no one formulation can be said to be typical of either period. The opinions of the governors past and present reflect not only state-to-state variations but also the governor's own interpretation based on his personal prejudices and convictions. Nevertheless, there seems to be common agreement on the principal functions of the governor. If these functions are considered together with the data on the time spent on each function, which are presented in the preceding section of this chapter, a reasonably accurate and realistic pattern of gubernatorial functions emerges.

In 1947 Millard F. Caldwell was serving the last year of his four-year term as governor of Florida. The campaign for his successor was about to begin, and he took the opportunity presented by a request to address the annual meeting of the Florida Chamber of Commerce to summarize his impressions of the duties of the governorship. The governor began his talk with an introductory comment to the effect that some problems were too big for one state acting alone to handle and that, therefore, the governor must work harmoniously with the governors of the other states. He then presented a "factual description of the powers and responsibilities of the Chief Executive of Florida," the major points of which are as follows:

> . . . A Governor's first responsibility starts with his campaign. The dominant party in Florida prepares no gubernatorial platform and the determination of the objectives to be followed during the succeeding four years is largely left to the candidate. The Legislature, by long standing custom, has adopted the practice of treating the successful candidate's platform as the public mandate. . . .
>
> After the Governor's election comes the duty of intimately acquainting himself with the details of administration and the selection of department heads and staff. The judgment evidenced by the appointments will determine whether the State will enjoy four years of politics or four years of capable government. . . .

. . . The Governor of Florida serves as Chairman and member of numerous Boards such as: The Budget Commission, The Board of Commissioners for State Institutions, The State Board of Education, The Department of Public Safety, The Trustees of the Internal Improvement Fund, The Board of Administration, The Pardon Board, The State Board of Pensions, The State Board of Conservation, The Board of Drainage Commissioners, The Labor Business Agents Licensing Board, The Agricultural Marketing Board and others. . . .

After the Governor has selected and appointed his official family, his next big job is to look to the future and prepare a four-year program to be incorporated in the message to his first Legislature. That session comes quickly on the heels of his inauguration and fast, careful work is necessary if his recommendations are to be characterized by feasible soundness.

One of the problems a new Governor will be interested in and will devote considerable thought to is the organization of the State administrative functions to the end that efficiency be improved and cost reduced. But, unfortunately, until one has served as Governor he is not qualified by necessary experience to recommend a far-reaching program of this sort, although incidental steps may be taken in that direction. He has not acquired the necessary knowledge to make his recommendations in time for the first session, and the second Legislature is generally unsympathetic to sweeping programs of a new order.[7]

Thus the functions of the governor of Florida may be summarized as preparing a platform for his campaign, preparing and presenting a four-year program to the legislature, acquainting himself with the details of administration, appointing his major department heads and staff, serving as chairman or member of numerous boards and commissions, and devoting thought to administrative reorganization.

In an interview, Governor J. Strom Thurmond (1947–51) described the duties of the governor of South Carolina as falling into six major categories. These may be briefly summarized as the execution of the laws, legislative leadership, membership on boards and commissions, appointments, pardon and parole (in conjunction with a board of pardon and parole), and acting as the representative of the state in dealing with other states and the federal government.

On the whole, the southern governors tended to emphasize the policy-making aspect of their duties, particularly their role as legislative policymaker. For example, former Governor R. Gregg Cherry of North Carolina (1945–49), in commenting on his first year in office, said that "The vast majority of my energies was spent in connection with the function of the General Assembly which was in session for the greater part of the first three months of the year."[8] Governor James E. Folsom of Alabama also emphasized this aspect of his duties. In a radio talk on the governor's functions, he asserted that the state's chief executive must "first recommend policies and programs to the legislature." Governor Folsom also viewed the governor's role in policymaking to include that of setting the policy of certain executive departments and recommending party policies.

In other sections of the United States, there was less emphasis by the governors on legislative relations and policy formation, but it was more a matter of emphasis than it was disagreement on the importance of policy formation. For example, Governor Johnson Murray of Oklahoma (1951–55), in one of his regular weekly radio talks to the people of Oklahoma, discussed his concept of the proper functions of the governor. In introducing his remarks he expressed sentiments that have been shared by most governors at the close of a legislative session:

> . . . In most departments of your state government, peace and quiet reign once more. Administrators and state workers generally are breathing easier. The reason for this sudden return to normalcy, of course, is the fact that the state legislature has gone home. After a hectic four and one-half months, its work is finished for another two years. . . .
>
> Which brings us to the job ahead. As I see that job, it is to administer all this new legislation in such a way as to benefit the greatest possible number of Oklahoma citizens. That job isn't going to draw as many bold-type newspaper headlines as the hot and heavy oratory from the legislature. But it's a lot more important. The *administration* of our laws is the final and supreme test of those laws. Good

laws, poorly administered, can sometimes become bad laws. By the same token, the wise administration of a poor law can make it into a good law. . . .

As I see it, the primary job of your governor is one of administration. . . . Up to this point, I have been involved almost exclusively in the legislative end of being governor. And I don't mind saying that it's going to be a distinct pleasure to get better acquainted with other aspects of the office. . . .

I intend to spend as much time as possible in months ahead doing what I consider two important things. First of all, I want to determine what the people of Oklahoma are thinking, what their problems are, and how they hope to overcome those problems. And the only way I know of to determine it is to get among 'em. . . . So, I intend to spend a good deal of time in informal visits in all sections of the state. As governor, it's my job to represent all the people. It's my opinion that I can represent them better if I know at all times what they're thinking and doing. . . . While touring the state, as time permits, I also intend to have a firsthand look at all our state institutions.[9]

A slightly different type of approach to the functions of the governor was taken by Sigurd Anderson, governor of South Dakota (1951-55).[10] Governor Anderson summarized the governor's functions under three heads. First, he said the governor must provide for the proper administration of state government by seeing that all the various officers, boards, and commissions operate efficiently. This involves supervision of those agencies under the governor's direct control and also the appointment of the proper individuals to carry out these functions.

Second, Governor Anderson said that the governor must provide guidance for the state government. He felt that this guidance could be provided in two principal ways. First, because the governor in South Dakota serves on a great many of the state's most important boards and commissions, he can provide personal guidance of the state's affairs through these agencies. Second, the governor must also ensure the enactment of his program by the legislature.

Third, the governor should "bring the government to the people." This was interpreted by Governor Anderson to mean that the governor should use various meetings, affairs, banquets, and personal interviews, as well as the press and radio to reach people. Governor Anderson said that he planned to institute a regularly scheduled radio program as one means of accomplishing this end.

A very interesting discussion of the governor's functions which gives a good deal of the flavor of actual operations in the forties can be found in an address by Governor Forrest C. Donnell, then governor of Missouri, to the National Governors' Conference in June 1943. The title of Governor Donnell's address, "The Usual Duties of the Governor," is indicative of his approach to the governor's functions. He began his address by stating that the two principal duties of the governor were the faithful execution of the laws and the recommending of measures to the legislature. "In connection with this duty," the governor said, "should also be mentioned the power of veto which, I believe, exists in the Governor in all but one of the states. The word 'Governor' is derived from a Latin word signifying 'to steer a ship.' The duty of recommendation by the Governor to the legislature of his state and his power of veto are important in enabling the Governor to steer, or at least to assist in steering, the ship of his state." The governor then went on to describe the governor's "usual" duties in these terms.

> When, however, each Governor here present shall, a day or a few days hence, have returned to his office in the capitol of his state, he will find himself confronted . . . with the *ordinary* business of his state which engages, day by day, a large proportion of his time. If the legislature of his state be in session, bills from that body will be upon or about to reach his desk and, in nearly every such state, each of those bills will require his decision as to whether it shall be approved or vetoed. Proceedings for the extradition of persons charged with crime will require his attention. Applications for pardons or paroles may be present or near at hand for his action. Flood conditions or threatened violence may present to him the necessity for each decision as to whether he shall call out troops of the State Guard for enforcement of the law, preservation of property, or protection of life. Vacancies in local offices, with petitions and letters from advocates or opponents of persons who seek appointment to fill those offices, may require of him early and discriminating attention. State administrative boards and commissions will have before them practical ques-

tions requiring prompt joint thought and action of their members, of whom he is one. Financial problems, perhaps of eleemosynary or educational institutions, will require his assistance and counsel. Methods of punishment in penal institutions of his state may be presented to him for study and decision. In addition, constantly arriving correspondence from constituents and others, on a variety of types of subjects, may necessitate early personal consideration and response by the chief executive of the State. In short, the Governor . . . will on return to his office resume . . . those more prosaic, but nevertheless extremely essential, duties which devolve upon him in the management of the ordinary current affairs of his state.[11]

The governor's views on their functions in the 1960s and 1970s were not greatly different from those in the 1940s and 1950s. For example, Governor Jerry Apodaca of New Mexico (1975-79) said in a personal interview that he felt that the governor actually had two constituencies. The first of these was the people of New Mexico and the second was the state legislature. He went on to explain that if the governor could not adequately serve the second constituency, he would not be able to serve his major constituency. This is simply another way of saying that the governor must be able to get along with the legislature if he is to get his program passed. He also said that, of course, the governor had to take care of the day-to-day operations of the government.[12]

Although Governor Apodaca did not mention public relations in his interview, it was clear that he made careful arrangements for media coverage. While visiting Sante Fe, I attended one of Governor Apodaca's press conferences and found that not only was the session covered by the members of the press but also by representatives of radio and television as well. Governor Apodaca used the session to make a number of announcements that he wished reported in the media and also answered numerous questions. While Governor Apodaca emphasized his legislative and administrative duties more than public relations, it is clear that all three of these functions were still a part of the governor's duties in New Mexico in 1976 just as they were when I interviewed the governor of New Mexico in 1956.

Governor Raul H. Castro (1975-77), who was governor of the

neighboring state of Arizona during the same period that Apodaca was governor of New Mexico, had a slightly different view of the governorship. He pointed out that the governor's principal function was to set the tone of the administration and to establish policy. However, he quickly added that it was really the legislature who established policy and that, while the governor could recommend, the legislature really had the final word in the matter. He said that he thought the governor had an adequate appointing power but he had considerable doubts about whether the governor's appointments should be confirmed by the senate.[13] Such confirmation, of course, usually has been considered one of our traditional checks and balances. However, it is easy to see how a governor who may have had some problems with the senate on recent appointments might feel differently about the matter. Governor Castro also pointed out that while the governor of Arizona appoints most of the principal officers of state government, he generally does not control the highway commission since it is appointed on staggered terms. This lack of control was regarded by the governor as an impediment to his role in policy formation. This view is also easy to understand, since at the time of the interview with Governor Castro, the highway commission was all Republican except for one Democrat. Consequently, as a Democratic governor, Castro may have had some difficulty in getting his highway programs accepted by the commission.

I think it is a fair summary of Governor Castro's views to say that he definitely believed that the principal function of the governor was to establish policy, appoint his principal department heads, and, in general, to run the government. However, as many governors have found, these powers are shared with the legislature; consequently, it is not a one-man show in any state.

The Center for Policy Research of the National Governors' Association in 1976 made a survey of the governorship, a part of which was devoted to the governors' functions. Because of the ground rules under which the study was conducted, the governors who replied cannot be quoted by name. Nevertheless, their comments are quite valuable as an insight into the actual functioning of the office. For example, on the question of public relations one governor wrote:

No area is more sensitive to the maintenance of good public relations for a governor, and conversely to creating unneeded ill will, than the responses made to written and telephonic communications addressed to the chief executive's office.

Accordingly, perhaps more personnel and more staff hours were devoted, in my administration, to creating and maintaining such a system than to any other single function of the office.[14]

As was pointed out earlier, the average governor in the 1970s received at least 500 pieces of mail each day and probably over 200 phone calls. Consequently, one important part of his public relations functions is the proper handling of mail and phone calls. The actual processing of mail and the handling of calls are the responsibilities of his staff. The speed and effectiveness with which they operate will of course reflect favorably or unfavorably on the governor. In an ideal situation the governor's staff should be so familiar with the governor's viewpoint on major issues that they can answer these letters and phone calls in the same fashion that the governor would.

It is beyond the scope of this study to examine the detailed composition of the governor's staff, but it is worth noting that several positions were found on the staffs of all the governors visited. In each office the governor had an executive assistant who was his principal staff person, although this individual goes by a number of different titles. In addition, there is a legislative liaison person, a position which reflects the governor's view of the importance of dealing with that body. A third staff member was the governor's legal counsel, a position that has not been touched on in this study but is quite important in terms of guarding the governor against legal errors. Another prominent staffer is the governor's press secretary, now sometimes called director of public information. Finally, there is the governor's appointments secretary who controls the governor's personal interview schedule and who approves all the governor's outside appointments and public appearances.

It should not be assumed that because these five positions were found in all governors' offices, this exhausts the list of staff members. In addition, in almost all offices there is a person who acts as a liaison to one or more of the major departments. In fact, in larger offices the departments were grouped, and the governor had a liaison person for every two or three major departments. In addition, in some governors' offices a special adviser on the budget is found. In most, however, there is no one person who is responsible for the budget since this is a function of the executive budget office. This office, in most states, is not actually in the governor's office, but it operates very much as though it were. In states where there is a good working relationship between the governor and the unit preparing the budget, the head of this office is one of the most important advisers to the governor.

In the late 1970s the median size of the governor's staff was around twenty-three professional members. However, even a median figure is somewhat deceiving, and it is difficult to draw generalizations about the governor's staff. For example, in 1979 the size of governors' staffs ranged in size from over eighty persons in California, where it is necessary to have a director of administration to supervise the staff, to no more than half a dozen in states such as Wyoming and Utah. While there is a rather direct relation between the size of the governor's staff and the population of the state, this relationship breaks down in the smaller states; because the governor must have a certain minimum number of staff members, he tends to have more than the population might warrant on a strict ratio basis. This is because there are certain functions such as relations with the legislature and the press and policy formation that must be carried out, and the governor needs sufficient staff to cover these functions.

It would appear from this description of staffing patterns that the formation of policy is not covered. However, this is not the case. In most offices, the governor's public policy functions generally are not clearly broken down within his staff. Questions of public policy, of course, are also questions of politics in the narrower sense. Consequently, the governor's chief adviser on "public policy" is likely to be his executive assistant or his principal political adviser in the governor's office. Also, the governor makes wide use of various department heads in preparing any sort of program. For example, it is highly unlikely that the governor would recommend an increased emphasis on farm-to-market roads without discussing his proposals with the highway director. In fact, a program of this nature is quite likely to be prepared by the highway department.

Depending upon the governor's policy on lobbying, the department might well be responsible for securing the adoption of the program by the legislature.

The governor's role in policymaking appears throughout his other functions. Consequently, he is assisted in his policy role by different staff members at different times. Thus it is difficult to separate out any particular staff member who advises the governor only on "policy." Occasionally there was a governor who did have a staff member responsible for one or more of the major policy projects that the governor had stressed in his campaign and actually expected to implement. However, this was the exception rather than the rule, and policy formation is one function in which the governor is quite active personally.

In selecting policy advisers or other key staff members, it is interesting to note that many governors do not feel that the persons who were on the governor's campaign staff are necessarily the best people for his office staff. One of the governors commented on this point:

> Without any question the most crucial aspect of an effective administration is the selection of the staff. Exceptional talent and loyalty are the most important considerations. Watch out that arrogance doesn't creep into staffers' manner when dealing with state agencies. Effective campaign workers often do not prove to be the best staffers. By way of warning, any governor in any state can drown in the details of state government and end up accomplishing nothing. He should select talented people to head agencies, give them broad responsibilities, back them up and save himself for major decisions.[15]

Several of the governors who were interviewed made the point that it was very difficult to accomplish more than a very few things in any administration. Their views apparently have fairly widespread support among other governors of the seventies. For example, Governor Jerry Brown of California (1975–) is quoted as saying that "There are only so many issues that the legislature can digest and there are only so many gubernatorial initiatives that the legislature can assimilate in one year."[16]

Another governor had basically the same view in relation to the development of policy. His advice to an incoming governor was:

Decide early what two or three things you want to accomplish; develop a sound public information program to let people know; and devise and constantly revise methods for evaluating your own performance, using outside sources.[17]

What this governor did not say was that while policy can be developed in the fashion he describes, any substantial change will have to pass the legislature. Consequently, relations with that body are certainly an important part of the governor's plans for policy development. It is interesting to note that the governor quoted above did stress the development of a sound public information program. As has been suggested before, the governor not only must have a good program but the people must know about it; they must be convinced that the governor is doing a good job if he is to be successful. A governor is judged not only on what he does, but on the people's perception of what he does. For this reason the public relations aspect of the governor's duties is quite important in shaping the way the people will view his functions in the area of policy formation.

The importance of the public perception of the governor's role was clearly reflected in a statement made by Governor Fob James of Alabama at a briefing held for the representatives of Alabama's smaller daily newspapers in January 1981. James started the briefing by saying that he had learned much about the value of public perception in his first two years as governor. He further explained the learning process by saying that "I didn't think you needed to work on public perception, but I learned that in public life, it's very important because the legislature is a reflection of it. I just thought you came down here [to Montgomery, the state capital] and went to work."[18]

This approach to public life was a logical one for James to have held because he is one of the new breed of businessmen-governors who tend to come into office with no previous political experience. Thus, the heavy emphasis on the need for public explanation on the part of the governor was a new development in his experience. However, the mere fact that the governor held a series of briefings on his proposed programs prior to the legislative session in Alabama in 1981 would seem to indicate that he now pays a good deal of attention to what he termed "public perception."

A somewhat different, but equally significant, version of the governor's role in public relations was that advocated by Tom McCall, a two-term governor of Oregon (1967-74). In part Governor McCall said:

> I think it is also important that a governor should strive to serve as a chief informational officer for the people. Because solving a problem is never as hard as gaining public awareness of and acceptance of the thesis of the problem, a governor should articulate the problems, sound warnings, clarify the suggested courses of action, elicit support from the people, involve private citizens and action groups, etc. In short, not only should he be the spokesman *for* the people, but he must also be a spokesman *to* the people. In a very real sense, his is a central communications desk, seeking to maintain order in advance, seeking to keep political avenues "open during remodeling."[19]

It is quite easy for the governor to become isolated from the public in spite of public appearances. For this reason the Center for Policy Research of the National Governors' Association recommends a rather interesting position which they call a "perspective keeper." They point out that, of course, no governor's staff has a position with such a title. Nevertheless, it is really necessary for the governor to have someone to act in this capacity even though that person may not be on the governor's staff. For example, one of the governor's college friends, a business associate, his wife, or others who are not seeking any public office or further political advancement are the best possibilities as "perspective keepers." Since they have no ax to grind, they will feel free to tell the governor what is on their minds. While their judgments may not be correct, they give the governor a fresh outside view, which is quite useful. Governors, as well as presidents, can sometimes suffer from being completely surrounded by their staff and protected from the facts of life. The larger the organization the more likely this is, but even in a small state a governor can develop a complete sense of unreality. Unless he has methods to revive his perspective, such as contacts with the average citizen or his "perspective keeper," he may well get a distorted view of any state problem.

Another interesting way to assess the governor's functions is to determine which functions the governors thought were the most difficult and which were the easiest. This approach was used in the questionnaires of the National Governors' Association and has been well developed in the study cited above. However, it was further refined by Thad Beyle in an article in 1979 in which he not only gave a summary of the governors' views on this matter but also advanced an interesting explanation of why some governors had differing views on the question.[20] Table 14 is based on the answers of some fifty-one present and former governors to the question of which of their duties they found the most difficult.

TABLE 14
THE VIEWS OF FORMER GOVERNORS ON THE MOST DIFFICULT ASPECTS OF THEIR OFFICE

Aspect	Percentage
1. Interference with family life	49
2. Working with the legislature	43
3. Ceremonial duties	41
4. The hours	35
5. Tough decisions	31
6. Invasion of privacy	29
7. Intramural government squabbles	27
8. Working with the federal government	24
9. Building and keeping staff	20
10. Working with the press	20
11. Management of state government	18

SOURCE: Adapted from Thad L. Beyle, "Governors' Views on Being Governor," *State Government* 52 (Summer 1979): 105.

An examination of the table reveals that there are three aspects of the office which emerge as the most vexatious from the governor's point of view although these aspects are not necessarily either the most time-consuming or the most important. Some 49 percent of the governors ranked "interference with family life" as the most bothersome aspect of their duties. This is quite understandable to anyone who has looked at the schedule of the governor, and it is clearly revealed in the tables presented earlier. One governor whom I interviewed previously had been a member of Congress. However, he felt that his position as governor was considerably more difficult than that of a congressman because of the vast demands on his time, which meant a sixty-hour week at the office and practically no time with his family. He contrasted this role with that of a congressman, which was difficult but did give him some privacy and a great deal more time for family affairs.

The emphasis which this study has put so far on the governor's relations with the legislature is also supported by the governors' views since they ranked it second. Some twenty-two of the fifty-one governors (43 percent) listed "working with the legislature" as the second most difficult duty. The third most difficult duty listed by the governors was their ceremonial, or public relations, functions, a duty which also had been stressed in the discussion of the functions of the governor. This probably does not mean that the ceremonial chores actually were particularly difficult but simply that they were time-consuming and onerous. On the other hand, one or two governors commented that they found ceremonial duties actually to be the easiest of their duties. Apparently ceremonial duties were placed in the "difficult" category by most governors because of the vast amount of time that they consumed. Most governors felt that this time could have been better spent on other duties such as policy formation or on their families. After these three, we find smaller percentages agreeing on the most difficult duties. The duties that rank next in line are the long hours, tough decisions, invasion of privacy, intramural governmental squabbles, working with the federal government, building and keeping staff, working with the press, and the management of state government.

It should be noted that there was a good deal of disagreement on some of these matters, which can be related either to the size of the state or the powers of the governor. For example, Beyle found that those governors who complained most about working with the legislature tended to be governors whose powers (as reflected in an updated version of Joseph A. Schlesinger's index of formal powers) fell in the moderate or low brackets. Among the powers on which the Schlesinger index is based are appointment, budget, tenure, and veto. All of these, of course, are useful in dealing with the legislature, and thus Beyle may have hit upon a valid explanation for these differences.

About the only thing that seemed to be related to party in any significant way was interference with family life. Sixty-one percent of the Republicans complained most strongly about this aspect of the governorship compared to only 39 percent of the Democrats. Beyle suggests that this difference may be due to the fact that more Republican governors, particularly in the seventies, tended to come into office with a limited background in government. Consequently, they did not really expect the tremendous pressure of their ceremonial duties, of the long hours, and of other matters, all of which add up to interference with family life. This explanation seems reasonable and probably applies not only to Republicans but also to Democrats who may come to the office from a business background. The so-called businessman governor, particularly one who has been successful and has run his own corporation, is most likely to suffer from the kinds of pressure found in the governorship. For example, it is unlikely that you will see a headline in the capital city newspaper to the effect that the president of the Easy Rest Bedding Corporation is in bed with the flu. On the other hand, the same individual when he becomes governor is quite likely to find himself in the capital paper under the headline "Governor in Bed with the Flu." Then will follow a detailed story quoting the governor's press secretary, his doctor, and almost anyone whom the reporter can find willing to comment on the effect of the governor's illness, its probable length, and its severity. It is a newsworthy instance because it affects the governor, and anything that affects the governor is newsworthy. This is the kind of thing that it is very difficult for a businessman, particularly if self-made, to understand. The businessman cum governor also frequently has very little taste for ceremonial duties. This falls in somewhat the same category as interference with family life because the ceremonial duties of the governor, as was previously pointed out, take up so much time that they do tend to interfere with family life.

In fact, working a sixty-hour week as governor of any state will interfere with family life. However, as one governor explained, "It all comes with the territory." Any governor who goes into office must expect to find that his time with his family is severely curtailed. Nevertheless, this time may be expanded through careful scheduling. One of the points stressed by many former governors when they give advice to incoming governors is that the governor should set aside a block of time each week for his family. This is good advice; not only does the governor need some time off but he also needs some time with his family because he is quite likely to be elected during his children's formative years. If he has teenage daughters and sons, he is particularly needed at home during this period.

The study made by the Center for Policy Research and Beyle's refinements add to our understanding of the burdens of the office of governor. However, the relative emphasis the governors put on the different aspects of their office are not always the same as those put on their functions by the governors. For example, the governors list interference with family life as the most difficult aspect of their office. While this is a very real aspect of the governorship, its number one ranking does not tell us anything about the relative importance of the functions the governor must perform. Rather, this ranking emphasizes the fact that the governor's functions collectively take a great deal of time and thus interfere with family life. Furthermore, many of the aspects of the office which the governors found to be difficult apply to one or more of his principal functions. For example, "working with the legislature," listed as second by most of the governors in terms of difficulty, also plays a very important part in policy formation. The "tough decisions" which the governors list as fifth may relate to either policy or administrative matters, but they are part of the policy process; many of them are what governors regard as "can't win" situations. There are actually a number of issues on which the governor must take a position but which have no politically sound answer. For example, on a pro-abortion bill there may be no really satisfactory answer. If a governor signs it, his action is sure to spark substantial criticism, but he will get an almost equal amount of criticism if he vetoes it.

The things the governors found easiest are not necessarily the least important. For example, they found the management of state government easy, as they did working with the press and building and keeping a staff. It is suggested that if they do build and keep an adequate staff, they will find working with the press and the management of state government less difficult than if they did not have such a staff. Many governors stressed the importance of a good staff, and it was previously suggested this is a significant factor in the governor's being able to accomplish his tasks.

In the chapter which follows we will pursue what seems to be the most important of the executive functions—the governor's role in policy formation. We will not try to cover the governor's role in public relations and management because these seem to be adequately set out in this chapter and in other studies of the governorship.

Notes

1. Martha Wagner Weinberg, *Managing the State* (Cambridge, Mass.: MIT Press, 1972), p. 45.

2. Ibid., p. 47.

3. Coleman B. Ransone, Jr., *The Office of Governor in the South* (University, Ala.: Bureau of Public Administration, 1951), p. 23.

4. Coleman B. Ransone, Jr., *The Office of Governor in the United States* (University, Ala.: University of Alabama Press, 1956), p. 137.

5. Center for Policy Research, *Governing the American States: A Handbook for New Governors* (Washington, D.C.: National Governors' Association, 1978), p. 50.

6. Ibid., p. 125.

7. Millard F. Caldwell, "The Governor's Duties and Responsibilities," an address before the thirty-first Annual Meeting of the Florida State Chamber of Commerce at St. Petersburg, Florida, 2 December 1947.

8. Raleigh (N.C.) *News and Observer,* 2 January 1946, p. 12.

9. These selections were taken from the text of the governor's radio speech recorded for broadcast at 6:45 A.M., Saturday, 26 May 1951. Italics are the governor's.

10. Interview with Governor Sigurd Anderson, Pierre, South Dakota, 10 July 1951.

11. Governor Forrest C. Donnell, "The Usual Duties of the Governor," an address before the National Governors' Conference on 23 June 1943, *Proceedings of the Governors' Conference, 1943,* pp. 118 ff.

12. Interview with Governor Jerry Apodaca, Santa Fe, New Mexico, 16 December 1976.

13. Interview with Governor Raul H. Castro, Phoenix, Arizona, 11 December 1976.

14. Center for Policy Research, *Governing the American States,* p. 50.

15. Ibid., p. 57.

16. John C. Bollens and G. Robert Williams, *Jerry Brown in a Plain Brown Wrapper* (Pacific Palisades, Calif.: Palisades Publishers, 1978), p. 112.

17. Center for Policy Research, *Governing the American States,* p. 85.

18. The *Tuscaloosa* (Ala.) *News,* 14 January 1981, p. 1.

19. "The American Governor in the 1970s," a symposium, edited by Coleman B. Ransone, Jr., in *Public Administration Review* 30 (January/ February 1970): 38.

20. Thad L. Beyle, "Governors' Views on Being Governor," *State Government* 52 (Summer 1979): 103-9.

4

THE GOVERNOR'S ROLE IN POLICY FORMATION

One of the most significant points to emerge from this study is that the governor's primary role is the determination of the policies of the state government. The effort made by the governor to secure policies acceptable to him involves him in an attempt to mold the policies of his party and to influence the policy decisions of the legislature. It is also instrumental in causing the governor to promulgate policies that he hopes will guide the executive branch of the government. This threefold aspect of policymaking is sometimes described by saying that the governor "wears three hats"; he acts as party chief, legislative leader, and the state's chief administrator.

These distinctions are partially valid and are useful in studying the governor's role in policy formation, but it should be pointed out that most governors do not seem to be conscious of these distinctions in carrying out their duties. The tendency to ignore the subtleties of these distinctions is probably due in large measure to the fact that the effects of almost any decision are felt in all three fields. For example, most governors, even in merit system states, make a great many appointments. Some of these are major appointments such as a department head or a member of an important board or commission, but the majority of them are less important. It is easy to see how a major appointment can be used to pay a political debt, to influence a particular group in the legislature, or to build favor with a powerful interest group. It is also obvious that the appointment of a department head or a commission or board member is exceptionally important in terms of the control of administrative policy.

What is not quite so obvious is that minor appointments, which are sometimes considered to be routine administrative decisions, also have considerable significance outside the field of administration or management. The effect of these decisions is felt particularly in the fields of party control, legislative influence, and public relations. Because of their repercussions in these fields, minor appointments are frequently more troublesome to the governor than major appointments. It is these appointments that are the primary concern of the party managers who seek to influence the governor's selection in order to strengthen party organization. These appointments are also significant because the average legislator is more concerned with securing one of the more numerous minor positions for one of his constituents than he is with influencing the governor's selection of a department head. Minor appointments in the aggregate are also quite significant in terms of public relations. This is particularly true of appointments which impinge upon what are usually regarded as local functions such as appointments to drainage districts, conservation districts, levee boards, or county fair boards. It is also true of appointments to local offices whose incumbents are normally elected by the people of the community concerned but which are filled on a temporary basis by the governor on the death or resignation of the incumbent. The cumulative effect of a series of "bad" appointments to such minor positions can create unfavorable public relations for the governor.

The governor's decision on minor appointments is only one of the many, so-called routine, administrative decisions that he must make during his term of office. The process of policy formation at the state level involves a series of decisions, large and small, by the governor over a period of several years. The cumulative impact of the governor's decisions during the course of his administration probably determines his effectiveness in all three aspects of his role in policy determination. Some decisions are at a much higher level and are much more dramatic than others. Certain of these can be dissected and found to impinge more upon administrative policy than party policy or more upon legislative policy than administrative policy. Even so, it is difficult and probably misleading to try to categorize the governor's decisions in policy formation as being entirely within any one of these fields. It is for this reason that the governor's role in policy formation will be considered in this chapter as a continuous process with decisions in any one field having definite policy implications in one or both of the other areas of policy formation.

The major distinction generally made by the governors themselves in discussing their role in policy formation is between party and/or legislative policy on the one hand and administrative policy on the other. While many governors stressed the importance of both aspects of their policy function, most of them gave greater weight to the party-legislative aspect as opposed to the management aspect. Most of the governors agreed that more importance was ascribed by the press and the public to the governor's role in legislation than to his role in management, particularly in the coordination of policy. However, not all governors were completely happy with this emphasis. For example, former Governor Dan Walker of Illinois (1972–78) felt that the emphasis, especially by the press, on the governor's record in securing the passage of his program in the legislature tended to force the governor to devote more time than was warranted to this aspect of his functions. As a result of this overemphasis on legislative achievement, the governor is unable to devote sufficient time to the management aspect of his duties—a facet which Governor Walker felt is at least equal in importance to his role in legislation.[1] In spite of the reluctance of some governors to play out the roles assigned to them by the popular conception of their functions, it is extremely difficult, in practice, for a governor to escape an emphasis on the policy aspect of his duties. Consequently, the formation of public policy primarily through legislative enactment is still the principal function of the modern American governor.

The Development of the Policy Function

The emphasis on the governor's role in policy formation is a fairly recent development in the history of the office. It has not been too many years since the governor could be characterized properly as a figurehead. This characterization is hardly true in most states today, for the modern American governor is an individual who commands considerable respect and who has a decided influence on the formation of policy. The rise of the office to its present status regarding policy formation is the result of gradual growth over a long period of time.

The first step in this direction was the early insertion in the majority of state constitutions of the seemingly innocuous provision that the governor should recommend a program to the legislature. Many of these provisions follow the wording of Section 3 of Article II of the United States Constitution. This section provides that the president "shall from time to time give to the Congress Information of the State of the Union, and recommend to their Consideration such Measures as he shall judge necessary and expedient." An examination of the debates in the Constitutional Convention leads us to believe that the Founding Fathers apparently did not envisage a chief executive who would be an executor of the laws only. Rather, they saw in the president an agent who would guide the deliberations of Congress by presenting to that body what he considered to be the major issues before the country at the time of his inauguration and "from time to time" during his term of office. In spite of the repeatedly expressed fears of the early state constitution makers of the possible abuse of executive power, they were willing to admit the usefulness of the executive as an agent who could recommend policies for the consideration of the legislature.

This early view that the executive not only can recommend but perhaps is expected to recommend a program to the legislature has been of considerable significance in the development of the American theory of executive-legislative relations. The fact that this power did not become fully effective until it was later implemented by other powers should not obscure the fact that the men who framed the federal and state constitutions hit upon a very significant concept. Their unhappy experience with government by committee in the Continental Congress and in some of the early revolutionary legislatures taught them that a large legislative body was not the best agency for sifting the many requests for action which confronted the state and national governments, even in that era of relatively limited government action. Consequently, the Founding Fathers provided for an executive who had the duty of sorting through the maze of conflicting demands and proposals and presenting to the legislature a program which he thought worthy of their attention.

Our concept of executive-legislative relations is based on the proposition that the executive *should* prepare a program. Here is the basis for the policy-forming function which is given so much emphasis in this study. If there were no provision for proposing policy, a much narrower view of the gubernatorial function, which would exclude policy formation, might be in order. However, this constitutional provision gives the governor not only the opportunity but also the duty to present a program to the legislature. The present emphasis on policy formation by the executive at the state level is an understandable outgrowth of this power and is to be viewed with approval rather than with suspicion.

The power to recommend was only the initial step in the development of the office to its present status in the field of policy formation. The next significant development was the provision for the selection of the governor through a statewide election. The importance of this development was obscured when it was first introduced by the fact that not only the office of governor but also offices of a number of other executive officers were made elective. This emphasis on the election of all executives frequently was coupled with a one-year term for these officials. These two Jacksonian concepts at first proved to be substantial impediments to the development of gubernatorial power. In the long run, however, the provision for the popular election of the governor was perhaps the most important single step in the governor's development as policymaker. Through statewide election, the governor was placed in position to speak for the people of the state as a whole in contrast to the legislature, which spoke with a voice representing many sections and many factions. This is not to suggest that the governor may not speak with the voice of a faction or a section. Indeed, there is considerable evidence to show that with the shift of the population in most states to the cities, he now speaks with distinctly urban overtones. In spite of this, however, the people seem to view the governor as a spokesman with a statewide viewpoint.

The development of the governor's role as the people's tribune has been very gradual and is much farther advanced in some states than in others. However, its growth has been accelerated in recent years for two reasons. One is the high caliber of men who have come to occupy the office. The second is the availability of modern means of communication that have enabled the governor to reach the people swiftly and directly. Thus he has been able to build up a backlog of popular support which is essential, if the situation warrants, for appealing to the people over the head of the legislature.

During the recent history of the office, many able men who were not content to act simply as the executor of the laws or to serve as a check on the legislature were elected to governorships. Each felt that his state faced one or more significant problems, and each attempted to see that his solutions were enacted into law. Statewide election had increased the prestige of the office, and the governors gradually were able to focus the attention of the voters on their role as a representative of the people. The development of first the press, later radio, and most recently television has aided the governor considerably in this endeavor. While these facilities are open to members of the legislature and to the other elected officers, the governor is in the best position to exploit the potentialities of the media. There are many legislators and sometimes a considerable number of elected officials, but there is only one governor. Many of the governors elected after World War I were colorful and dynamic personalities and were able to utilize the media to build up a powerful following among the voters who, of course, were also constituents of the legislature. Many of the successful governors of the modern period have not hesitated to carry their program directly to the people in the case of conflict with the legislature. In most situations, however, the daily media coverage is simply used to build general public support for their programs whether or not their legislatures are in session.

In addition to his media coverage, the governor in most states has been given the power to appoint an increasing number of state officeholders. Appointments to minor posts can be used as patronage and hence are sometimes useful in dealing with the legislature. However, the increased scope of the gubernatorial appointing power at the top level of administration probably has been of more significance in the governor's attempts to establish policy, particularly within the executive branch itself.

Added to these powers was the fact that by the beginning of the present century the governor had been given the power of veto in every state except North Carolina. This power considerably improved his position vis-à-vis the legislature and has been used to good effect in most states. However, as is pointed out in a subsequent section, it is generally a power which is used only after other methods of dealing with the legislature have failed. Furthermore, while it represented an important additional weapon in the governor's arsenal of persuasive powers, it does not seem entirely logical to maintain that this was the key factor in the governor's rise as a legislative policymaker. To do so is to ignore the fact that the governor of North Carolina, who was not given this power, apparently has been reasonably successful in his dealings with the legislature of that state.

In the last thirty years the governor has been given the sole power to prepare the budget in all but three states. This power is of great significance in policy formation. In addition, the governor now has the added clout of a four-year term in almost all states. This longer period not only strengthens the governor's hand in policy formation but the opportunity to succeed himself, now possible in most states, means that he is likely to serve another four years.

The modern American governorship, as a result of the seven factors mentioned above, has developed into a position of considerable importance and relatively high public esteem. These factors include the power to recommend legislation, statewide election, acceptance as the people's tribune, increased appointing power, the addition of the veto power, the development of the executive budget, and increased tenure potential. The contemporary governor has been able to capitalize on his increased power in his efforts to secure the passage of his key policy bills by the legislature.

The governor's role in policy formation began in the area of legislative policy formation, since it was in this area that he was first given effective powers. At the same time the governor began to develop as a party leader largely because the same powers which enabled him to deal effectively with the legislature also enabled him to become a political leader in his own right. His statewide election focused upon the office the attention of the voters and resulted in his legislative program receiving considerable popular endorsement. The office gradually became the central focus in state elections and became a sought after position in terms of political preferment.

The governor became a spokesman for his party and the leader of his party in the legislature. His powers of patronage and veto could be used not only to secure the passage of legislation but also to build a political following within his own party. The governor's emergence as a party leader seems to have paralleled his emergence as a legislative leader. In a way he was forced into party leadership in an attempt to secure the enactment of his legislative program. Over and above this aspect of party leadership, the governor in many states also became a party spokesman for his state in party councils at the national level. The governorship then gradually returned to its post-revolutionary prominence as a stepping-stone to higher political office, and many candidates for the presidency and a large number of senatorial candidates have come from the gubernatorial ranks. Thus, the forces which tended to give the office a legislative orientation also helped to develop the governorship as a locus of party leadership.

The role of the governor in the establishment of administrative policy followed his emergence as a legislative and party leader in the states as a whole and has grown to an effective level only in those states where administrative powers have developed sufficiently to enable him to operate as a leader in administration. In most states the administrative aspects of his role in policy formation have not yet been fully realized. In spite of the theory that the governor is the state's chief executive, his powers in the executive branch in a majority of the states are not fully developed. Consequently, the governor seeks to formulate policy in those areas where such policy will be successful. At the present stage of the governorship in the majority of the states, those areas remain party and legislative policy.

The emphasis which we find on legislative policy formation has been partly forced on the governor by the state legislature itself. Not only have the legislatures frequently proved inept in their attempts at policy formation but they also have demonstrated a definite tendency toward restricting the governor in the execution of the laws. Many state constitutions and most state statutes are characterized by an overabundance of detail. As the structure of state government became more complex, it also became more difficult to understand. Consequently, state legislatures seem to have developed the view that not only the policy control of the government but also the administration of the laws would slip from their grasp unless the governor and his department heads were rigidly controlled by statute. Hence, the statutes setting legislative and administrative policy began to be laid out in great detail. A governor coming into office with a program involving any real change in the status quo is immediately faced with the fact that the implementation of his program will require one or more of the following: (1) changes in already existing legislation, (2) the passage of new legislation, (3) a change in the current allocation of funds by the legislature, or (4) new taxation if the policy change requires a level of expenditures that is beyond the scope of current revenues. Any or all of these efforts will require the cooperation of the legislature whether the changes be in substantive legislation or in the appropriations bill. Consequently, if the governor expects to make major changes in policy, his first moves tend to be in the field of legislation.

Since the governor prepares the budget in most states, this power can be used to highlight many of the policy changes which the governor wishes to see enacted. The governor's budget message, therefore, is a policy document of considerable importance in all but a few states. In three states, however, the governor is not solely responsible for the preparation of the budget. In Mississippi the governor is ex officio chairman of the commission on budget and accounting. However, it is this body and not the governor which has the authority to prepare the budget. The same pattern is found in South Carolina where the authority rests with the state budget and control board, which is under the governor's chairmanship. In Texas the authority to prepare the budget is given both to the governor and to a legislative budget board so that there are, in practice, two budgets prepared for each fiscal year. In those states which have a system of budgeting by board or commission, the budget does not necessarily represent the governor's views and consequently is not as important a policy document from the governor's point of view as it is in states with an executive budget. Even in those states without the executive budget, however, the governor attempts to incorporate in the budget as many of his policies as possible and frequently incorporates in his general message to the legislature those policies that he could not persuade the budget commission to accept.

It should also be pointed out that in many of the forty-seven states which have an executive budget, the budget document seldom reaches the high goals set for it as a policy device. One of its primary limitations is the fact that the budget actually covers only a part, sometimes as little as one-fourth, of the state's income and expenditures. This is true because in many states the majority of the state's income derives from revenues earmarked for predetermined purposes.

Another limiting factor is the poor timing of the budget. In many states it must be submitted shortly after the governor takes office and before he has time to make a thorough analysis of the major policy problems involved. Frequently much of the governor's substantive program, which should have been a part of the budget, must be presented later in the session. These and other limitations reduce the effectiveness of the budget as the central focus in the process of policy formation. Nevertheless, it is an important part of the overall process in a majority of the states.

Policy Planning for a Legislative Program

The initial role which the governor will play in forming legislative policies in his state is conditioned to some extent by the political setting. For example, in the one-party states, the governor has a free hand in the formation of his platform, which presumably serves as the basis for his legislative policies. In a one-party state, the party has no platform except those of the individual members of the party who are running for office. The real contest is in the primary. In this contest the platforms of the candidates for the governorship, for the other elected executive offices, and for the state legislature represent the views of the candidates and need not, and usually do not, contain similar policies. As a result, when the primary is over and the winners are known, the platforms of the winning candidates for office are not necessarily related. The party itself has had no platform in the primary, and since the general election is a formality, it develops no platform in that contest. Under these circumstances, the governor in a one-party state starts out with the advantage of having a platform that actually represents his real policy positions.

In the normally Democratic and Republican states, the governor is in much the same position, since he is actually elected in the primary, and the platform on which he was elected is one of his own choosing. In the general election that platform may be changed slightly to conform to the party's concept of what its program should be in the succeeding four years. However, most of the planks will be those taken from the platform that the gubernatorial candidate used in his successful primary campaign.

In a two-party state, the governor may have to accept further alterations in the name of the party because the platform must be one on which an entire slate of candidates, including the state legislators, can campaign. However, the governor in his campaign is free to choose the issues that he will stress or ignore and thus runs primarily on a platform of his own making.

The governors of all states, therefore, go into office with a platform of sorts, much of which was developed by the gubernatorial candidate and his advisers. In the one-party states and in the normally Republican or Democratic states, the governor has a somewhat freer hand in the exact provisions of the platform. In all states, however, the platform will tend to reflect enough of the governor's major policies so that it will form a satisfactory basis for operation if he actually desires to implement this program.

The actual effect of the party platform on the process of policy formation is not entirely clear and varies greatly from state to state and within a given state from one campaign to another. Most party platforms are deliberately vague documents which are long on high-sounding objectives and short on the actual policy for reaching those objectives. Hence, during the first legislative session following a governor's election, he generally redefines the platform by selecting a few issues to be presented to the legislature in his first message. In addition, changes in the state or national political or economic scene may bring to the fore issues that were not crucial during the campaign itself. On some occasions entirely new issues are presented in the governor's messages. Generally, the governor's program is further refined in practice by the fact that not all of the bills introduced at the governor's request will actually receive full gubernatorial support. For political reasons it may be necessary for the governor to advocate certain policies in his messages and to have bills introduced that embody those policies. His real program, however, will consist only of those bills that actually are pushed with all the resources at the governor's disposal. In the final analysis, the governor's program will embody only a part of the party platform and may, in addition, contain measures which are not mentioned in the platform at all. The party platform is a part of the policy-forming process only to the extent that some of its planks find their way into the governor's real program.

The mechanics by which a "gleam in the governor's eye" becomes a concrete proposal that can be put before the legislature for consideration vary considerably from state to state. Some of the major agencies used for research and bill drafting include the governor's immediate staff, the budget agency, the regular departments of government, the agents of interest groups, and the facilities of the state educational institutions. Although legislation is influenced by interest groups whose legislative representatives probably prepare some "administration" measures, it is difficult to determine just how much of the governor's program originates with these sources. Certainly some measures may be attributed to interest group activity, but probably a smaller part of the governor's program should be attributed to these groups than frequently is credited to them, especially by members of the press.

While many pressures are brought to bear on the governor, some of these pressures are directed toward influencing the governor's administrative policy rather than his legislative policy. For example, a highway contractor who contributed heavily to the governor's campaign is certainly interested in seeing that the governor emphasizes a program for the construction of new highways. However, the contractor is much more interested in securing the contracts for equipment or supplies for those highways that are constructed. It is quite probable that both candidates for the governorship had a highway construction program that would be acceptable to the contractor. His primary interest lies in doing business with the administration in power. This type of thinking is characteristic of many interest groups that are more interested in patronage than policy as long as the governor maintains the status quo on policy matters and does not advocate rash action, such as a moratorium on new highway construction or a cut in schoolteachers' salaries.

In addition to whatever use the governor may make of interest groups, he also has available the services of research units at state universities. While some governors take advantage of these resources, other chief executives view academics with suspicion and make little use of their services.

In some states certain members of the governor's staff are quite influential in determining the content of the policies that they draft for the governor, while in others the staff members are used more for technical assistance in drafting legislation than for advice on its policy content. Here also the actual part played by staff members in influencing the governor's policy determinations is difficult to determine. In general, staff members play a substantial role in policy determination if for no other reason than the fact they are in constant touch with the governor and, hence, are in a position to influence his decisions through their recommendations on policy matters both pending and proposed. Since the organization of the staff and the determination of its duties are at the discretion of the governor in most states, responsibility for the preparation of legislation that is delegated to staff members does not follow a fixed pattern throughout the states. In most states this responsibility is not placed on any one member of the staff, although in several states the governor has a special legislative secretary or legislative assistant.[2] However, the primary function of this individual generally is not so much to prepare legislation but to keep the governor informed of what is happening in the legislature and to push those bills which the governor favors and block those that the governor opposes. The person in this position also may be responsible for the clearance of legislation proposed by the executive departments.

Policy formation during a governor's term does not operate as a one-way street. When the newly elected governor takes office, particularly when this represents a change in political parties, he is generally forced because of lack of time and lack of confidence in the personnel already in office to have most of his program prepared by the members of his own staff or by confidential advisers, who may be entirely outside the government. However, by the time the governor reaches the second legislative session in his term, most of his administration bills are likely to be the product of the departments under his direct supervision. The governor cannot be an expert in all fields, and if he has confidence in the ability of a department head in a given field, he tends to accept his suggestions for changes in the existing program or for new programs. The increasing technicality and complexity of legislation in many fields of state government reinforces this tendency to rely on department heads. A great many of the governor's legislative proposals, therefore, originate with a department head and are drawn up by the staff of the department concerned. This insures their technical adequacy and assures the governor of the assistance of whatever interest groups the department can muster to assist in securing passage of the legislation.

Out of this complex of the governor's personal desires, the party platform, the work of various research agencies, the planning of the budget agency, the prepared programs of interest groups, the work of the governor's staff, and legislation prepared by the governor's own department heads come the major pieces of policy legislation. No definite pattern seems to emerge as to the relative importance of the contribution of each of these groups to the overall program. However, in the case of a newly elected governor, major reliance generally is placed on his own staff, with some assistance from advisers either within or without the government for the preparation of his initial program.

Presenting the Legislative Program

Several of the governors interviewed pointed out that a newly elected governor is at a considerable handicap in attempting to present a carefully prepared program to his first legislature because of the brief period for preparation. The primary problem is the poor timing of the initial session of the legislature after the date of the governor's election. The typical pattern is for the governor and legislature to be elected in early November in one year and some to take office only slightly over one month later in early January of the succeeding year. In a majority of the states the first legislative session is also early that same January. This pattern gives the governor very little time to prepare his legislative program for his first legislative session. Even though most governors now have a four-year term, the timing of the first session of the legislature still presents a definite problem. The governor is at the height of his powers and probably at the zenith of whatever goodwill he may expect. Consequently, his first session is an important opportunity for him to establish the policy directions of his administration. If he fails to do so in the first session, it may be much more difficult to mount major policy initiatives in the remaining sessions, especially if the legislature meets only twice during his term.

The governor in a one-party state is in a somewhat more favorable position for program planning than is the governor of a two-party state. While technically a governor in a one-party Democratic state is elected in November and must present his program to the legislature, which generally meets in January, he is actually elected in the primary which is usually held in May, July, or August. Thus, the successful candidate in the primary has a period of from four to seven months in which to plan his program.

Of course, there is nothing to prevent a candidate in a two-party state from preparing a carefully worked out program which he can hold in readiness in the event that he is elected. However, it is difficult to work out such a program in the heat of a political campaign. Consequently, it seems reasonable to give the governor at least two months, after he is in office, to prepare a program because there are a number of other problems to which a newly elected governor must give his attention in his first few weeks in office. Among other things, he must give prompt attention to major appointments and must deal with the horde of well-wishers and favor-seekers who flood his office. Two months are a minimum period for the governor to prepare a budget and a comprehensive legislative program.

In formal recognition of the separation of powers theory, the governor and his department heads do not participate in the proceedings of the state legislature as they would under a cabinet form of government. This formality, however, is no bar to the introduction of the governor's major pieces of legislation. In fact the same constitutions that prevent the governor from taking a direct part in debates in the legislature generally provide that he shall, "from time to time, give to the legislature information on the state of the government, and recommend for its consideration such measures as he may deem expedient.'' As has been pointed out previously, provisions of this type not only permit but require that the governor make recommendations to the legislature. The only power which is lacking is that of actually introducing the legislation. In most states with an executive budget, this minor omission has been remedied in regard to financial legislation. The governor's budget message actually is submitted to the lower house of the legislature as a concrete proposal and frequently by statute must contain a draft of the proposed appropriation bill.

In any event, the introduction of legislation is the easiest step in the process of policy formation as far as the governor is concerned. In the two-party states the governor has access to the floor of both houses in the person of the leader of his party in each house. This is also generally the case in the normally Democratic and Republican states, where it is customary for the two parties to have leaders in each house. In the one-party states there is usually no formal party organization, but the governor secures the introduction of legislation through a friendly legislator or through an individual who is known as "the governor's floor leader," whose functions are discussed in some detail in a succeeding section.

The Governor's Batting Average

In most states the measures embodying the governor's program are known as "administration bills." This designation ordinarily does not give the bill any official standing but in some instances the bills based on the governor's budget are given a preferred position. In most instances, however, administration bills are no different from other bills in so far as the rules of the legislature are concerned. In practice, the designation of the bill as an administration bill does have great significance in connection with its actual position in the order of business and with its passage.

The American governor in the past seventy-five years has had considerable success in obtaining the passage of administration bills embodying his major policy proposals. No overall box score on the number of administration measures that have been passed is possible because detailed studies of executive-legislative relations in the respective states, which would be necessary to compile such a presentation, are not available. However, on the evidence which is available, the governor's success is quite marked. For example, a study of legislative action on specific recommendations made in the governor's messages during the regular sessions of the Alabama legislature in the early 1940s revealed that over 71 percent of the governors' recommendations were enacted into law.[3] No similar studies have been made since that time, but interviews with several more recent Alabama governors reveal that they credit themselves with a success rate between 50 percent and 100 percent. The record of Governor Fob James (1979-) in his first legislative session in 1979 appears to have been an exception to this general pattern of success. There were three major facets to Governor James's legislative program—the construction of new highways to be financed from a proposed four cents a gallon tax on gasoline, the complete revision of the constitution of Alabama, and a program for a war on illiteracy for which the governor recommended an appropriation of $20 million. The gasoline tax never made it out of committee, the constitution passed the senate but was bottled up in the house committee on constitutions and elections, and Governor James was able to get only one-half of the $20 million he wanted for his war on illiteracy. Thus Governor James's record of success in percentage terms would only be about 17 percent. This does not compare favorably with an overall success rate of the governors of Alabama since 1940 of about 70 percent.

However, these figures are a graphic illustration of the results when a quantitative methodology is applied to what is essentially a qualitative problem. Recent governors of Alabama might have done better with the legislature than Governor James, at least in percentage terms. However, none of them tried to raise the gas tax in a time of sharply rising gasoline prices or declared war on illiteracy at a time of escalating education costs (though most strongly supported education), nor did they try a complete revision of the Alabama constitution. By almost any standards the revision of a state's constitution and an increase in the gas tax are significant programs that are exceedingly tough to pass. To be sure, the governor got less than one-third of his programs through the legislature. However, can we be confident that a half of a war on illiteracy is not worth more than the 17 percent "success rate" assigned to it?

What is lacking in our 17 percent success rate is any suggestion of a qualitative measure. Consider for a moment the fact that if a completely new constitution had been passed, it would have been worth no more than 33.3 percentage points. Yet had the constitution passed, Governor James would have accomplished something that would have to be considered a major feat in Alabama politics. The qualitative problem is significant and cannot be dismissed with the pat statement that "the data are not available." However, this real deficiency in the study of state politics will not be overcome until data that are qualitative as well as quantitative are available. These data must be from a broad enough sample of states over a long enough time span to give us the basis for a better judgment than can presently be made on the success of the governor in getting his program through the legislature.

In the meantime, Governor James may want to take heart not only because the 17 percent quoted above may not actually measure his success with the legislature but also because he is not the first governor who lost the battle for a gasoline tax. Over thirty years ago a governor of Vermont suggested that the batting average approach did not tell the whole story. The governor noted that he had been successful in securing the passage of twenty-two out of twenty-seven administration bills giving him a batting average of 81.5 percent. However, he pointed out that the five on which he was defeated were very important. In particular he felt that the legislature's failure to increase the motor vehicle and gasoline tax in order to raise sufficient funds to meet available federal grants for highway construction was a major defeat. The governor said that repercussions from this failure were already reaching his office in the form of delegations from various sections of the state, telephone calls, and letters, complaining about the lack of proper highways.

If history repeats itself, Governor James may look forward to delegations who want highways built with nonexistent funds. Also, it would appear that it would take at least ten years before an attempt can be made to evaluate the results of the war on illiteracy. However, governors of Alabama can serve for only two successive terms, so Governor James may have to wait for the verdict of history on his education program. Furthermore, it is highly unlikely that the other three sessions of the legislature in 1980, 1981, and

1982 will produce such traumatic results for Governor James. A long tradition of strong governors in Alabama is on his side, and most governors do learn from experience.

These two illustrations some thirty years apart in two states half a country apart geographically and at least that politically are undoubtedly only two of many hundreds of examples in which the qualitative aspect of a governor's program goes unmeasured. It is quite possible that the qualitative aspect of the measures on which the governor was defeated may have outweighed the quantitative aspect of those measures on which he was successful. Statistics on the governor's batting average, therefore, are no infallible guide to judging the governor's success or failure as a legislative policy-maker. However, they are the best index we have at the present time of the governor's ability to get his major programs through the legislature.

Another possible weakness in using quantitative data is that the program which the governor presents to the legislature may be tailored to fit the kind of proposals which the governor thinks that body may enact. This, however, is one of those imponderables that cannot be taken into account in a statistical presentation. Furthermore, this approach on the part of some governors may be balanced by a tendency on the part of other governors to present a much more ambitious program than they feel the legislature will pass. By so doing they hope to put the legislature on the spot in the public's mind for the failure of the governor to live up to some of his more exaggerated campaign promises.

In spite of the caveats stated above, the statistics available on the governor's relations with the legislature indicate that the governors were successful in pushing their programs through the legislature in the 1940s and early 1950s. In addition to the previously cited Alabama average of 70 percent plus, the governor of Tennessee in 1947 had a success rate of almost 50 percent, while the governor of Kentucky had an outstanding 96 percent batting average. Virginia, a state where the governor is traditionally strong, shows impressive statistics ranking from a low of 50 percent to a high of 96 percent.

Gubernatorial success in this period was not confined to the South and to the border states. For example, in 1951 Governor Walter J. Kohler, Jr., of Wisconsin, in his closing address to the

joint session of the legislature, summarized the success of his legislative program by stating that: "I can report to you that of the 55
pieces of legislation specifically recommended by me . . . 47 have
been enacted into law. . . . " Thus by the governor's calculations,
a very respectable 85 percent of his administration bills had been
passed by the legislature.

The governors' batting averages have declined in the 1960s and
1970s although they have not declined as much as might be expected
in view of the increase in divided party control. As was pointed out
in Chapter 1, there has been a sharp increase in the last twenty years
in divided party control at the state level. Thus it is now quite com-
monplace for the governor to be faced with one or both houses
controlled by the opposition party. It would seem logical, therefore, to expect the governor's batting average to decline in those
states; this did occur, as illustrated by at least one study in the late
1960s.[4]

In this study of a representative sample of ten states during the
legislative sessions of 1966, Alan S. Wyner found that his data supported the proposition that the governors' success in the passage of
administration bills closely correlates with his party control of the
legislature. The governor had his greatest success in those states in
which his party controlled both houses of the legislature, but this
success rate falls when his party loses control of one house and
drops even lower if his party controls neither house.

In view of these findings, it is somewhat surprising to find that
the governor in 1966 was still batting a respectable 71 percent in the
passage of administration bills in the ten states examined. In view
of the continued increase in divided party control since 1966, it may
be that the average would drop lower if the period 1966–80 is examined in depth in all fifty states. However, this is a hypothesis that
still remains to be proved although it may be considered a logical
extension of Wyner's findings and is certainly in accord with my
own limited sampling based on interviews.

The Veto

The pattern of success suggested above is reinforced also by an
examination of the other aspects of the governor's relations with

the legislature. For example, another device which may be used in roughly measuring gubernatorial power vis-à-vis the legislature is to examine the success with which the governor has been able to make his veto effective. If an examination of the ability of the governor to get certain proposals through the legislature is accepted as a positive measure of his strength, then the ability of the governor to make his veto stick might be called a negative measure of his strength. An examination of the relevant data shows that the American governor has been remarkably successful in this aspect of executive-legislative relations.[5] While the use of the veto has varied greatly from state to state in the course of the history of executive-legislative relations, its greatest use and effectiveness have been in the twentieth century. About three-fourths of the total number of vetoes of legislation by the governors have occurred since 1900. This has been due in part to the fact that during the present century the volume of legislative business has increased substantially.

It is interesting to note that the average percentage of bills vetoed has remained about the same over the last 30 years. For example, in 1945 the ratio of bills vetoed to bills passed was a relatively low 5.1 percent. Some thirty years later in the legislative sessions of 1975 and 1976, it was an almost identical 5 percent.[6] Thus, there has been little change in the rate at which the governors of the states have vetoed legislation. However, there has been more of a change in recent years in the governors' ability to sustain their vetoes. In 1945 the governors' vetoes were overridden by the legislatures only 1.05 percent of the time, and more than one-half of these were in Wisconsin. On the other hand, in the regular sessions of the legislatures in 1975–76, some 6.8 percent of the bills vetoed by the governors were passed over their veto.

Thus, the percentage of bills on which the governors' vetoes were not sustained has risen slightly over 5 percentage points in the thirty-year period. However, as is usually the case in working with aggregate data covering forty-nine states, overall summaries conceal about as much as they reveal. For example, during the 1975–76 legislative sessions, all of the governors except the governor of Nevada vetoed one or more pieces of legislation.[7] However, the governors of some states were much more active in the exercise of this power than others. For example, the governors of four states—California (332 vetoes), New York (312 vetoes), Illinois (217 vetoes), and Maryland (175 vetoes)—accounted for 49.9 percent of all gubernatorial vetoes during this period. However, in spite of the number of the governors' vetoes in these four states, only in Illinois were any vetoes overridden. In that state the conflict was fairly sharp, but even there only 26 of the governor's 247 vetoes were overridden by the legislature for a fairly respectable 10.5 percent rating. In most of the other states the governors did not veto as large a number of bills as in the four states cited above but their record in having their vetoes sustained was good. During the 1975–76 sessions there were only twelve states in which the governors' vetoes were overridden. The percentage of overrides ranges from a low of about 4 percent in Kansas to a high of almost 86 percent in West Virginia.

Consequently, the picture presented by using overall figures differs sharply from the picture presented when using a finer state-by-state breakdown of the fate of the governors' vetoes. In overall terms, it is quite accurate to say that in thirty-seven of the forty-nine states no vetoes were overridden and that the overall ratio of vetoes overridden for the forty-nine states was only about 6.8 percent. On the other hand, it can also be accurately stated that in those states in which vetoes did occur, the governors had considerable problems in persuading the legislature to uphold their vetoes. The governor did well in Kansas, where only 3.7 percent of his vetoes were overridden, and the governor of New Hampshire did fairly well, where only 5.8 percent were overridden. However, the governor's record was much worse in Massachusetts (73.3 percent) and in West Virginia (85.9 percent). The overall average of vetoes overridden was 28 percent in those states in which vetoes occurred.

Consequently, while the governors did extremely well in general in their attempts to see that their vetoes were not overridden, any evaluation based on aggregate data must be tempered with a note of caution to the effect that in a given state with a given legislature, the governor's record may not be impressive. Also, we should note that his "control" over the legislature is not quite what it was from 1930 to 1950. Nevertheless, "control" is a relative matter, and for the governor to make his veto stick 93.2 percent of the time in the states as a whole during the 1970s is not a shabby record even if it is 5 percentage points behind that in the 1940s and 1950s. Also, it must be remembered that in many states the governor's veto is so effective that it is a rarity for a bill to be passed over it. For example, in California prior to Jerry Brown's ascension to the governorship, it was possible for a student of that state's politics to say that "no gubernatorial vetoes have been overridden since 1946 and only a few have been seriously contested."[8] In California over the period from 1915 to 1965, the governors of California vetoed about 11 percent of the bills that passed the legislature. The trend appeared to be downward in the latter part of this period since Governor Goodwin J. Knight (1953–59) vetoed 8.2 percent of the bills sent to him while his successor, Governor Edmund G. (Pat) Brown, Sr. (1959–67), vetoed only 7 percent of the bills passed. However, this trend was reversed under Governor Ronald Reagan (1967–75) and Governor Edmund G. (Jerry) Brown, Jr. (1975–). Under these two governors the veto rate went to 13.4 percent in the 1973–74 legislative sessions and back to 11.9 percent for the 1975–76 sessions. The overall ratio of bills vetoed to bills passed over the last four administrations in California is thus about 10 percent. This veto rate would put the California governors in a "high use" category but still below such states as New York or Illinois.[9]

Virginia is another state in which the pattern of support for the gubernatorial veto is well established. Compared to their counterparts in California, however, governors in Virginia appear to be quite restrained in their use of the veto. For example, from 1952 to 1956 the governor vetoed only 1.2 percent of the bills passed, and none were repassed over his veto. From 1968 to 1977 the percentage of bills vetoed went up to 3.3 percent, and all of these vetoes also were upheld.[10]

The analysis which has been made of the governor's batting average and the corollary analysis of the exercise of the veto do not furnish conclusive proof that the governor is a successful legislative policymaker. Most of the evidence, however, does seem to point in this direction. While in some states there is a tradition of weak gubernatorial leadership in the last thirty years, these states now seem to be in a minority. It also is true that even in states which have a tradition of strong gubernatorial leadership, there are occasionally governors who are completely ineffective in a policy-forming role. On the whole, however, the average governor in the United States in the past thirty years has proved to be a legislative policymaker of no mean stature. This policy, however, is not made in a political vacuum, and the governor cannot function effectively as a policy leader unless he can secure the support of a working majority of the legislature. It is to the governor's relationship with that body that the next section of this chapter is devoted.

The Nature of Executive-Legislative Relations

One of the most interesting aspects of executive-legislative relations revealed by this study is the substantial degree to which these relations depart from what frequently is regarded as the ideal pattern at the state level. Certainly from the governor's point of view the ideal situation is one in which both the governorship and a majority of both houses are controlled by the same party. This pattern is, in fact, accepted as typical by many scholars of state politics. The governor in dealing with the legislature, therefore, is supposed to work through the leaders of his party in each branch. His program is supposed to be based on the party platform and, consequently, receives the support of the members of his party in each branch of the legislature. The party, therefore, serves as a coordinating device to produce harmony in the relationships of the two branches.

While on the surface this description may seem to fit the facts in most states, an examination of the actual political situation in those states shows that such a pattern is the exception rather than the rule in more than half of the states and, therefore, cannot be regarded as typical. As has already been pointed out, about one-fourth of the states fall in the one-party Democratic category, so that the governor, upon his election, can rely on an overwhelming majority of his party in both houses of the legislature. On the surface this follows the ideal pattern, since both the governorship and the legislature are controlled by the same party. Actually, such control in party terms is meaningless. In a one-party situation there can be no successful appeal by the governor to party solidarity because there is no opposition party. There is no party platform because the party is simply a holding company for competing factions. The platform on which the governor was elected is his own and usually has no relation to the platform on which the legislators were elected so that they do not necessarily feel bound by it.

In these states the ideal pattern simply does not fit, because there is no opposition party to perform its necessary functions. The governor in dealing with the legislature is dealing with factions, not parties. Generally, these factions are transient groupings which change with the issues before the legislature. Sometimes, however, the factions are fairly consistent throughout a legislative session. When they seem to be fairly stable, they are most often found in the form of a pro-governor and an anti-governor clique. Most of the interviews conducted in the course of this study support this assertion, but some of those interviewed saw the factions in their state as primarily rural-urban splits in the legislature. These splits were likely to continue from governor to governor and were not formed in reference to the policies of any particular governor. This sort of rural-urban split seemed particularly prevalent in the normally Democratic states.

Legislative factionalism is not confined to one-party states but seems to be equally typical of the normally Democratic states. In these states the majority of the dominant party in the legislature is usually substantial, although not as great as in a one-party situation. Here the governor may be able to call upon the legislators in the name of the party to support his program, but the effectiveness of this appeal is diminished considerably by the lack of a really challenging opposition. The major party generally is broken up into factions, and the governor's strength comes largely from one faction of his own party. Sarah McCally Morehouse's analysis suggests that the governor's faction is based on continuing support from a group of legislators that can be traced back to the primary in which the governor was first nominated.[11]

Not all gubernatorial factions, however, are made up primarily of members of the governor's own party. In some situations his strength is drawn from a faction of his own party plus a part or all of the opposition party. This is particularly true when the governor is a liberal and a substantial number of his own party are conservatives or vice versa. In the first case, the governor seems to draw his strength from the liberal wings of both parties and is opposed by the conservative faction in his own party as well as by the conservative faction of the opposition party. The reverse is true with a conservative governor who draws his strength primarily from conservative legislators regardless of party.

The situation in Virginia during the legislative sessions in 1976 and 1977 is a good illustration of this kind of factionalism. The governor during these sessions was Mills E. Godwin, Jr., who was elected as a Republican but was considered by some to be in reality an extremely conservative Democrat. Therefore, since both houses were Democratic there was, at least on the surface, a situation where a Republican governor was facing a Democratic house and senate. As has been previously pointed out, this is not an uncommon situation in a normally Democratic state. Alexander J. Walker analyzed the vote in the senate on each of the motions to override a governor's veto. Walker's analysis is related to what he called "real veto/real controversy" bills. These are bills in which the veto had an ideological dimension and which provoked considerable debate and sharp division as judged by key floor votes. For the purposes of this analysis, the Democratic senate members were classified as moderate-liberal Democrats or as conservative Democrats while the few Republicans in the senate were not further classified.

Even though there was a Republican governor and a Democratic senate, none of the governor's vetoes were overridden. However, the significant point for our purposes is that the "conservative" Democrats voted with the governor 52.7 percent of the time, but the "moderate-liberal" Democratic senators voted with him only 17 percent of the time. Interestingly enough, a majority of the Republican senators voted against the governor's vetoes almost 74 percent of the time. "This," Walker says, "is probably a result of the fact that Republicans are still more likely to represent moderate and/or urban constituencies."[12] As Walker points out, however, the Virginia senate had so few Republicans during these sessions that their votes were not a major factor; the principal ideological differences were between the two wings of the Democratic party. This explains in large part how a Republican governor with a very conservative bent can draw enough strength from the conservative wing of the Democratic party to sustain his vetoes even with all but one or two of his own party voting against him. Patterns not unlike the Virginia situation are found in other normally Democratic or

Republican states. Also, except for the party labels, such divisions are found in the factional politics of the one-party Democratic states as well.

This brings us back to our original contention that the ideal relationships between the governor and the legislature do not really exist in most of the states. As was pointed out in Chapter 1, in over one-half of those states where there allegedly is real party competition, there is a division of party control. In these states the governor belongs to one party and one or both houses are controlled by the other party. Consequently, there is grave doubt that the party can perform its function as a coordinating device, simply because it cannot coordinate what it does not control. It would seem, therefore, that a more realistic view of executive-legislative relations might be based on the premise that the governor will either deal with individual legislators or with factions as is the case in the one-party or normally Democratic states, or that he will deal with one or both houses controlled by the opposition party as is frequently the case in the two-party states.

The concept that the governor must deal with legislators on an individual basis or as a bloc is not new. However, it is certainly worth more emphasis than it is sometimes given in discussions of party control and executive-legislative relations. The governor must deal with individuals or blocs in his own party in the one-party states because there is no effective opposition party. He must deal with individuals or blocs of his own and occasionally of the opposite party in the normally Democratic states because his own party dominates the legislature to a marked degree; the opposition, because of its relatively small size, is not effective in party terms. Even in most of the two-party states, the governor cannot deal with his own party as a unit, because that party does not control both houses of the legislature. Consequently he must deal with the opposite party or with a bloc of individuals in the opposite party in order to secure the number of votes needed to get his program enacted. Of course, there are situations in the two-party states in which the governorship and the legislature are controlled by the same party and where, given some party discipline, the governor may be able to make an appeal to the legislators on the basis of a party program. These situations, however, tend to be infrequent. The American governor must concern himself with building legislative support from among clusters of legislative factions. In only a few states does the party actually play its traditional role.

If we approach the governor's role in legislative policymaking as a process which must be carried on in the context of factional politics, then his role becomes one of seeking to build support wherever he can find a suitable power base. The basic problem facing the governor is to build a legislative bloc that will enable him to have his program enacted into law. This bloc may have as a base the members of his own party in the legislature, and in a real two-party situation the governor may be able to use his position as party leader to control enough votes to enable him to put through his legislative program. However, this situation seems to be the exception rather than the rule. The governor certainly cannot operate in this manner unless his party controls both houses. In many states this is not actually the case and, hence, the governor must deal with a faction of the opposing party in order to get his program enacted. In the one-party states the governor faces a body which is made up almost entirely of members of his own party who are loyal neither to the party nor to the governor and who must be dealt with either individually or on a factional basis. Consequently, it would seem that the governor in most states must begin upon his election, or preferably even before his election, to build up a bloc on which he can rely to support his legislative proposals. In the following section some of the methods open to the governor to build such support will be considered briefly. The methods in general have been widely discussed and, hence, need not be covered in any great detail here; an attempt will be made to illustrate the influence cycle which seems to exist in most states.

Methods of Influencing Legislation

The methods that a governor employs to secure the passage of his legislative program or the defeat of those measures inimical to his program vary from state to state and also within the same state under successive governors. In general, however, there are a number of methods, with steadily increasing degrees of pressure, that are used in an influence cycle to affect each important piece of legislation.

The first step in this cycle actually takes place prior to the legislative session in the caucus of the majority party in a two-party state or in informal meetings of the various legislative factions in a one-party state. In these caucuses or meetings the selections are made for the important posts of speaker of the house, president pro tem of the senate, the chairmen of important committees, and, in states with two functioning parties, the majority leader in each house. The governor is vitally concerned with this process because the fate of his program will depend on the treatment it receives in the legislature, and this treatment in turn depends primarily on the actions of the individuals who hold these important positions. If the governor is adept at politics, he will have his nominees for these posts selected and their subsequent election or appointment assured long before the first meeting of the legislature.

The speaker and president pro tem are formally elected by their colleagues in the house and senate. This, however, presents no real obstacle to an alert governor-elect who, if he has any semblance of strength in the legislature, will be able to secure the election of members of his choice to these important posts. If he cannot, it probably is indicative of a rough road ahead in his relations with the legislature.

In most state legislatures, the committee chairmen and committee members are appointed by the speaker of the house and either the lieutenant governor (as president of the senate) or the president pro tem of the senate. These officers, if they are supporters of the governor, will make sure that individuals friendly to the administration are selected for important committee posts and thus insure prompt and friendly consideration of important administration measures in committee. This is vital to the passage of these measures, for the state government, like the national government, is largely government by committee. The fate of important bills usually is decided before they reach the floor, and, in fact, it is only by favorable committee action that they will ever come before the legislative body for consideration. Hence, the governor must concern himself with all phases of the legislative process. He cannot be content simply with drafting legislation or even with having it introduced by a friendly legislator. If he is to see his program enacted into legislation, the stage must be set with a careful organization of the legislature, which runs from the presiding officers down to the individual committee members. This "interference" by the governor in legislative affairs probably was not foreseen by those who drafted the early state constitutions, but it has come about as a necessary corollary to the governor's role in policy formation.

The governor in a two-party state, if his party controls the legislature, is in a more favorable position vis-à-vis the legislature than his counterpart in a one-party state, since he has access to the legislature through the presiding officers in both houses and also through the majority leader in each house. These individuals are supposed to work with the governor on party measures and to represent his point of view in the legislature. In a one-party state, on the other hand, there is no formal party organization, but the governor still needs a channel to the legislature. This channel generally is established either through the speaker of the house, the president pro tem of the senate, or through an individual who is known as the "governor's floor leader." This individual does not occupy an official party position. He is selected by the governor from the prominent leaders in each house and is frequently the chairman of a key committee such as the finance committee. He is expected to represent the governor's views on measures before his house of the legislature including administration bills and bills proposed by individual members. The legislators who make up the governor's faction look to the floor leader for guidance in much the same way as members of the majority party look to the majority floor leader in a two-party situation.

The intraparty politics involved in the selection of the speaker of the house, the majority leader, or the governor's floor leader are sometimes quite bitter, and the scars which result may have an important influence on the ability of the governor to get his program enacted into law. For example, in a situation in which the governor and a majority of both houses belong to the same party, it is possible that the governor will become involved in the election of the speaker of the house. Sometimes he is forced to throw his weight behind one of the candidates for the office in order to secure the election of a speaker with whom he can work. Even if the candidate backed by the governor wins the election, the house member who opposed him is quite likely to become the leader of a faction of the majority party that is opposed to the governor. This faction, if it is joined on key votes by the minority party, may be strong enough to be decisive in a close vote. If the candidate backed by the governor loses in his race for speaker, the governor should be prepared for a long and difficult legislative session since no friend of his will be in the speaker's chair. The governor's role in the selection of legislative leadership is a very delicate matter in most states, since the legislature is inclined to regard this as interference in legislative affairs. Yet, the governor has a very real interest in the selection of these important officers and must attempt to make his weight felt without giving offense to the legislature.

The second step in the influence cycle is the presentation of the subject matter of the proposed legislation as a part of the governor's message to the legislature. This at least makes the legislators aware of the fact that the governor does have a concrete proposal in a particular field so that they can recognize the bill, when introduced, as part of the governor's overall program and know that it will be backed by the governor's considerable legislative powers. The fact that the governor presents his message to the legislature in person tends to highlight the importance of the program, since it is widely summarized and discussed in the press and on radio and television newscasts. The program is brought to the attention not only of the legislature but also of the people of the state as a whole. Consequently, the governor's program as presented to the legislature becomes a document of considerable persuasive power because of the attendant publicity. The legislators are aware that their constituents are informed of the governor's program and may ask embarrassing questions about the legislator's failure to vote for the program. Hence, the legislator has reason to support the program if only because its existence is well known to the folks back home. On the other hand, when word of the governor's program gets back to the legislator's constituents, they may deluge him with requests to oppose certain of the governor's proposals. The chances are good, however, that the reaction of the legislator's constituents will be favorable in most instances. This is the case because many of the proposals probably were part of the governor's platform that had been endorsed recently by a substantial number of voters in the general election or primary.

This popular endorsement has more effect than that usually credited to it. Several of the legislators who were interviewed pointed out that unless they were opposed violently and personally to a measure in the governor's program or were certain that their constituents were, they would support the governor's program since it had been approved recently by a large number of the state's voters. The average American legislator, while acutely conscious of the views of the folks back home, is not bent on sabotage of the governor's program simply for the sake of sabotage. Consequently, there are a good number of measures on which general approval can be secured without resort to strong pressures and sometimes without great effort on the governor's part.

There are, of course, many situations in which this generalization is not true. For example, in a two-party state when one or both houses are controlled by the party opposing the governor, it is sometimes true that the legislators, motivated by partisan considerations, do engage in what certainly looks like sabotage for the sake of sabotage. The same thing is sometimes true in a one-party state when the governor is of one faction of the party and a majority of the legislature is of another. Most of the legislators, however, seem to be far less inclined to be obstructionists than they are sometimes represented to be.

Sooner or later, however, one of the governor's proposals will be viewed by a legislator or a group of legislators as being personally obnoxious, opposed to the best interest of their constituents, or unacceptable to their faction. At this point the influence cycle usually comes into its third phase, which is based primarily on persuasion. In these situations, one of the most effective methods which the governor can use is a conference with an individual legislator or a group of recalcitrant legislators. This group may be a party caucus, or it may be the leaders of a faction. In the conference it may not be necessary for the governor to promise anything tangible in the way of patronage or other rewards. Frequently, the prestige of the governor's office coupled with a forceful presentation of his views may be all that is necessary. Most legislators are well aware of the governor's additional persuasive powers which he can use if forced. Therefore, it is probably fair to say that this knowledge, plus the prestige of the governor's position as chief executive and in some instances as party chief, tends to maximize the effectiveness of his arguments.

Of course, there are some situations in which a tremendous amount of pressure is brought to bear on individual members of the legislature. This is particularly true in situations in which party or factional control of one or both houses is very close or where one house is not under the control of the governor's party. In these situations, the governor may need only two or three votes in one or both houses to get his administration bills passed. In circumstances such as these, the governor may be forced to go a step or two further and swing the vote of a reluctant legislator through the promise of patronage and the threat of veto. On occasion, he might go so far as to veto a measure in which a particular legislator is interested because the legislator had refused to go along with the governor on an important bill. As was suggested in Chapter 1 of this study, it is in situations such as these that a vote becomes a vote whatever its party or factional origin. The political infighting to get an administration measure passed when its fate hangs on one or two votes may not be pretty but it seems necessary.

The rather plaintive complaint of a Kentucky legislator when faced with this sort of nitty-gritty situation is an excellent illustration of how the process looks from the legislative side of the fence. To understand the situation in Kentucky during this time period, it should be pointed out that Louie B. Nunn had just been elected in 1967 as the first Republican governor in modern times. Both houses of the legislature, however, remained under Democratic control. Thus when the governor introduced a sales tax bill, it seemed to be in for tough sledding. However, the bill was passed by the house. How this feat was accomplished is the subject of a revealing article by Kenneth Loomis, a staff writer for the *Louisville Courier-Journal*. The article was by-lined from Frankfort, Kentucky, the state capital, and was headlined "Legislators Explain Nunn's Fiscal Arm-Twisting." Since much of the flavor of Kentucky politics comes through in this description, it is quoted below almost in its entirety.

When the 5 percent sales tax bill left the House for the Senate yesterday, unscathed after being subjected to a multitude of amendments and two days of fervent oratory, it marked a victory for Republican Gov. Louie B. Nunn and GOP representation in the lower chamber.

But it couldn't have been done without the Democrats.

During the five hours of oratory yesterday, Rep. Norbert Blume, D-Louisville, explained how 57 Democrats can match votes with 43 Republicans and lose:

"Last night, many an arm was twisted."

One that was twisted is fastened to Rep. William Cox, Democratic freshman from Madisonville. He drew applause from both parties when he took time to explain on the floor how the power of the governor's office is traditionally used in Kentucky to capture votes on key issues in the legislature.

Tuesday, Cox supported the food-medicine-clothing amendment to the sales tax bill. Yesterday, in a vote to reconsider the amendment, he opposed it. He explained why:

"Today, each of us must vote for what we think are the best interests of our people," Cox said. "Yesterday I let my emotion and dedication to my Democratic colleagues override my sense of responsibility to my district."

Cox represents Hopkins County. He told the House that buried among the thick pages of appropriations in Nunn's $2.47 billion budget bill are projects for Hopkins County that total some $1 million.

Included are $500,000 for an area vocational school, $330,000 for a community college, $75,000 for airport improvements, plus money for tuberculosis and mental hospitals in Hopkins County.

Although Cox did not say it, all legislators know that the governor holds the power of "line-item veto" over the budget that will cross his desk. He can approve the whole document by signing it, but he can also veto any simple appropriation with a short pen stroke.

"When you receive much, much must be given," Cox said. "While I know enactment of a 5 percent sales tax will impose a considerable burden on some of my constituents, I know they are the ones who will benefit most from this budget. . . . "[13]

While it is true, as the story above illustrates, that, on occasion, arms must be twisted, it should not be assumed that this is necessarily the normal state of affairs in executive-legislative relations. Since the political situation varies sharply not only from state to state but even within a state, generalizations about the normal state of executive-legislative relations are dangerous. However, a reasonable hypothesis would be that as the unfavorable aspects of the state political situation become dominant or as the opposition to a particular measure increases, so also does the frequency with which such high pressure techniques as patronage and the threat of veto are used. In many states amicable relations were found between the executive and legislative branches of the government, and the governor was able to get his program through primarily by using the first three steps in the influence cycle.

Most legislators expect the governor to have a program, and they expect him to push that program. Even legislators of the opposing party understand this as a part of the governor's functions and are willing to go along to a considerable extent. In one of the southwestern states where the governor was faced by a majority of the opposite party in both houses of the legislature, the speaker of the house, the acknowledged leader of the opposition party, complained that he found it difficult to cooperate with the governor because the governor had not proposed a concrete program. In his view, the governor had been remiss in one of his most important functions, and the speaker was rather bitter about this dereliction of duty. The governor, the speaker said, should have known better, since he had been a member of the legislature himself. While this view probably is not typical of the attitude of opposition leaders toward the governor's program, it is indicative of the fact that most legislators, even of the opposing party, expect the governor to have a program.

The first three steps in the influence cycle seem to follow a general pattern in most states. The first step is the organization of the legislature, which is followed by the introduction of the subject matter of proposed legislation by the governor in his messages. These two steps in turn are followed by individual or group conferences with legislators to explain the governor's program and secure their support. If these three steps fail, then the governor may resort to other methods, and the steps in the cycle will not follow necessarily in any particular order since the influence used must be tailored to the situation at hand. Among the more common methods used are the threat of veto and patronage. The latter may take the form of the appointment of a legislator's protégé to a government position or the promise of a future appointment to the bench or some other position for the legislator himself. It also takes the form of awarding contracts to a firm in which the legislator is interested or paving certain highways and even private roads in the legislator's district. Occasionally, the governor will use his pardoning power as a lever in influencing legislation, and will pardon a legislator's constituent in exchange for the legislator's vote.

Clearly some of these methods leave much to be desired in terms of political ethics. However, a governor's use of patronage or the threat of veto to build a legislative bloc seems to be one of the realities of political life. While much can be done by the governor through the prestige of his office and through personal contact with the legislators, there may come a time when certain legislators must be dealt with differently. The use of such methods is disavowed by many governors who rightly stress what can be done inside the legal framework. Yet, there is much truth in the observation of one practicing politician that "you have to have votes to get your bills through the legislature and if you don't give the boys what they want you won't get the votes."

The necessity for building a bloc in the legislature is not always easily accepted by a new governor, particularly of the "businessman" variety. Most of these anti-politician types are naive about the process of governing and feel that the legislators ought to agree with them without further persuasion on measures that the governor sees as clearly in the public interest. However, when the governor is faced by a well-organized opposition, whether it be party or faction, he must build a better machine if he is to defeat that opposition.

The governor, even in merit system states, has a considerable number of appointments at his disposal and has considerable influence over such matters as highways and contracts in most states. If he uses some of this power to repay political debts from his campaign or to smooth the path of his program in the legislature, he has ample precedent for his actions. There is a long history of the use of such methods by former governors, which is understandable in view of the practical necessity of securing the enactment of a program, sometimes under very adverse political circumstances. The chances seem better than fifty-fifty that the governor will have as good a concept of the public interest as the members of the legislature. Since these members are selected from single-member districts, they tend quite logically to vote in favor of what they think are their constituents' interests or in support of interest groups that helped finance their campaigns. In such circumstances, there may be considerable justification for the governor's use of his power.

Even if a governor sticks to his belief that it is undesirable for him to use methods such as patronage to influence the passage of legislation, there are still other ways in which his influence can be exerted. One of these methods is the attempt by the governor to build public support for his program through direct appeals to the legislators' constituents. This method has become increasingly effective with the improved coverage by the press and radio and by the wide use of television. Many governors use weekly or biweekly radio or television programs to explain to the people the major issues before the legislature and their position in regard to those issues. Other governors use a daily or weekly newspaper column for this purpose. Added to these means of direct access to the citizens are the press conferences held by most governors. These press conferences, called usually at the governor's initiative, are generally attended not only by newspaper reporters but by radio and television journalists as well.

While all of these avenues of communication are open to the legislature as well as to the governor, the governor's position as the state's chief executive is of incalculable value in his contest for the public eye and ear. No single legislator or even a group of legislators can hope to command the audience which the governor can simply because of his position. Any governor gets a tremendous amount of free publicity during his term of office. Not all of this publicity will be favorable, but if the press, radio, and television representatives are handled properly, the governor finds himself with very effective channels to the voter. The net effect of all this publicity on the legislator's constituents has not yet been accurately determined, but many governors feel that it at least results in a favorable climate of opinion for their proposals.

Another device at the governor's disposal in most states, which can be used to center public attention on particular aspects of his legislative program, is the special session. The power given the governor to call a special session of the legislature has its origin in the belief that certain emergencies might arise, such as war, invasion, or economic collapse, which would make it desirable for the legislature to meet at some time other than that regularly appointed by the constitution. As a matter of practice, real emergencies are fairly rare. However, the business of government is pressing enough so that the governor may feel compelled to call special sessions to handle certain issues. In some instances the special session is used deliberately as a device to influence legislation.

The chief value of the special session as a means of influencing legislation is the result of two factors. First, the subjects to be considered are the governor's choice; second, the media's attention is focused on these particular issues. The governor in calling a special session centers the attention of the state on the problem or problems for which the session is called. Thus the legislature is placed in the position either of acting on these proposals as the governor wishes or of taking the political consequences, which can be serious if the electorate is concerned with the problem before the session. In some states the governor has the sole authority to designate the subjects which may be considered at the special session, and no other subjects can be introduced. In several states the stringency of this provision is relaxed by the fact that the legislature by an extraordinary majority can take up subjects beyond those specified in the call for the special session. In these states a special session frequently becomes simply another session of the legislature, and in practice many matters are taken up which were not suggested by the governor in his call for the session.

The fact that the governor has authority in many states to limit the subjects to be considered in a special session gave rise to the interesting problem of whether the governor might be impeached at a special session called for another purpose. This situation actually occurred in New York, where the impeachment of Governor William Sulzer took place in 1913 during a special session which he had called for the transaction of other business. The courts in New York took the view that impeachment was a judicial and not a legislative process; hence, the impeachment was constitutional.

The influence cycle in its final phase comes down to the use of the veto and in some states to the use of the executive amendment. Generally speaking, these are methods of last resort, since neither of them ordinarily is used until the governor's other resources for influencing legislation have been exhausted. Of the two powers, that of executive amendment, which is called the "amendatory veto" in some states, seems to be a more positive approach to the governor's role in the legislative process. Its principal advantage over the veto is that it enables the governor to make suggestions for changes in legislation instead of simply vetoing a bill.

As has been pointed out previously, the governor has been very successful in making his veto effective. Less than 7 percent of the governors' vetoes are usually overridden. Hence, the governor has a powerful negative voice in legislation when he chooses to exercise this power. Because state legislators understand the effectiveness of the veto, it is a powerful conditioning factor in securing legislative cooperation. The majority of overrides occur in situations where there has been a complete breakdown of executive-legislative relations and point to the fact that this power is used as a last resort. In normal circumstances the governor does not have to use his veto, for the legislature generally is willing to adapt legislation so that it can be passed without the risk of a veto. The veto, therefore, has not been listed as the last of the governor's powers for influencing legislation because it is unimportant. On the contrary it is quite important and is basic to many of his other powers. However, it does seem to come last in point of time; generally it is used only when other methods have failed.

If this analysis of the importance of the veto power is correct, it is difficult to explain the governor's leadership in North Carolina, where the governor has no veto power. While the governor of North Carolina has not been as effective a legislative leader as some governors of other states, it would not be fair to say that he has been ineffective. Most of the evidence on administration bills and the comments of local observers reveal that he has been effective in getting his program through the legislature. An examination of the situation in North Carolina shows that the governor uses all the methods that have been discussed to secure the passage of legislation except for the veto. A twofold explanation may be advanced to explain the governor's success in spite of his lack of the veto. First, the legislature seems to have developed some sense of responsibility; there can be no buck-passing of undesirable legislation to the governor with the knowledge that he will veto the bill in question and thus take the burden from the legislature. Secondly, the governor seems to have made very effective use of the legislative powers that he does have and his considerable powers in the field of finance to backstop his legislative powers.

There remains the interesting possibility that the governorship might have developed in other states to its present status even if there had been no veto power. It is difficult either to prove or to disprove this proposition with only the example of North Carolina. It seems that the importance attributed to the veto in the states as a whole is based on a sound analysis of the actual development of the office in those states. On the other hand, it certainly is true that the office of governor in North Carolina is not the weakest in the nation by almost any standards that might be chosen. The governor of North Carolina generally is a much stronger legislative leader than his counterpart in neighboring South Carolina, where the governor does have the veto power. It is obvious, therefore, that the development of the governor as a legislative leader cannot be attributed entirely to the veto power.

As this analysis has attempted to bring out, the governor's power to recommend was basic to the development of the governor's role as a legislative leader. This power, in itself, would not have resulted in the present importance of the governor's activities in the field of policy formation had not the office and its powers undergone other important changes. One of these changes, which enabled the governor to take a more meaningful part in the policy process, was the increased prestige that gradually became attached to the office. This was in part the result of the introduction of the system of statewide election as the method for selecting the governor. It was also due to the higher caliber of the individuals who have served as the governors of many of the states, particularly since World War I. In addition, the governor gradually began to build his legislative influence through such devices as the "organization" of the legislature, the judicious use of patronage, special sessions to center public attention on certain aspects of his program, and appeals to the people of the state. Also in all the states except North Carolina the veto has been a backstop to other methods of influencing legislation.

Notes

1. Summarized from the remarks of Governor Daniel Walker who served as the commentator on a panel on "The Contemporary Governor" at the Thirty-Seventh Annual Meeting of the Midwest Political Science Association, Chicago, Illinois, 20 April 1979.

2. For other examples of staff members who are used by the governor in legislative research and policy formation, see Chapter 3.

3. The figures on which this estimate is based are taken from Hallie Farmer, *The Legislative Process in Alabama* (University, Ala.: Bureau of Public Administration, 1949), pp. 167–84.

4. Alan S. Wyner, "Gubernatorial Relations with Legislators and Administrators," *State Government* 41 (Summer 1968): 202.

5. Frank W. Prescott's pioneering studies of the executive veto give useful insights into this aspect of executive-legislative relations prior to 1950. See particularly: "The Executive Veto in American States," *Western Political Quarterly* 3 (March 1950): 97–111, and "The Executive Veto in Southern States," *Journal of Politics* 10 (November 1948): 659–75. The figures cited in this section on vetoes prior to 1950 are from these articles unless otherwise noted.

6. The percentage for 1975–76 was calculated from data in *The Book of the States, 1978–79* (Lexington, Ky.: Council of State Governments, 1978), pp. 36–39. The data on overrides are from the same source.

7. The governor of North Carolina is not included in these calculations since he has no veto.

8. Willis D. Halley, *Should California Pocket the "Pocket Veto"?* (Berkeley: Institute of Governmental Studies, 1966), p. 8.

9. The data on California from 1915 to 1965 are taken from Halley, *Should California Pocket the "Pocket Veto"?* p. 4. Data on Governors Ronald Reagan and Jerry Brown were calculated from *The Book of the States, 1976–77* (Lexington, Ky.: Council of State Governments, 1976), pp. 60–62, and *The Book of the States, 1978–79* (Lexington, Ky.: Council of State Governments, 1978), pp. 36–39.

10. Alexander J. Walker, "The Governor's Veto Power," *University of Virginia Newsletter* 54 (December 1977): 2, and Robert J. Austin, "The 1978–79 Virginia Assembly: End of a Decade," *University of Virginia*

Newsletter 55 (September 1979): 1. The data on veto overrides are from a letter to the author from Austin dated 21 November 1979.

11. Sarah P. McCally (Morehouse), "The Governor and His Legislative Party," *American Political Science Review* 60 (December 1966): 923–42.

12. Walker, "The Governor's Veto Power," p. 4.

13. Kenneth Loomis, "Legislators Explain Nunn's Fiscal Arm-Twisting," *Louisville* (Ky.) *Courier-Journal,* 7 March 1968, sec. B., p. 4. Quoted by permission of the *Courier-Journal.*

5

THE CONTEMPORARY GOVERNORSHIP

There have been a substantial number of changes in the governorship in the 1970s as compared to the governorship as it existed in the 1950s. It certainly is not clear what these changes portend for the 1980s but it is interesting to speculate on what they will mean for the governorship.

This chapter will not attempt to cover all the changes suggested in the first four chapters of this book but will concentrate on five changes which seem to be of particular significance: (1) A shift in political party dominance in the United States at the state level, discussed below under "The Changing Political Environment"; (2) The widespread occurrence of divided government in which the governor is of one party and one or more houses of the legislature are of the other party; (3) A marked shift from a two-year to a four-year term, accompanied by the fact that the governor is actually serving longer in office than ever before; (4) The sharply increased cost of running for governor; and (5) a shift in the functions of the governor, who may become more an administrator than a policymaker. Although the governor's three principal functions of policy formation, public relations, and management remain the same as in the 1950s, the governors of the seventies have given more emphasis to their functions in management. This raises the question of whether the governor is becoming more of an administrator than a policymaker and how this shift might translate into future operations during the eighties.

All of these changes have subsidiary points that could be developed at length but will be subsumed under them in our rather short summary discussion. For example, there has been a shift of political parties at the state level in the general direction of the Democratic party with the demise, at least for the time being, of what used to be solidly Republican states. This shift has contributed to the divided party control which is discussed below. Divided party control also raises the question of whether the governor's veto now is less potent than it was in the fifties. If this pattern of divided party control continues and spreads in the eighties, it raises the possibility that the governor's power vis-à-vis the legislature will be diminished in the next decade.

The central problem raised by the increase in the cost of campaigning also has its subsidiary questions. For example, it raises the question of the significance of the role of the political consultant and of the impact of television in the selling of candidates. All of these subsidiary points can be touched upon only briefly here but have been discussed in more detail in the first two chapters of this study.

The Changing Political Environment

It is clear from the discussion in Chapter 1 that important shifts have taken place within many states in party control over the governorship and the legislature. The question of what may happen in the future is too intriguing to be left alone, but an attempt to answer it is not without its dangers. In matters political our hindsight is generally better than our foresight, and expected changes do not happen and changes that were not expected take place. Consequently, predicting is a perilous business at best. For example, in an article that I wrote in 1964 dealing primarily with the status of the governor in the South, there was a section at the end rashly labeled "The Next Decade."[1] In that section several predictions were made as to the role and status of the southern governor in the sixties.

Fortunately, more than three-fourths of these predictions were supported by developments in that decade. However, only about one-half of the predictions in regard to gubernatorial politics have been supported by subsequent developments. The principal prediction was that "we may expect what will be for the South a revolutionary change in voting behavior at the gubernatorial level. Republican opposition in gubernatorial races should grow and it is not unlikely that the next decade will see the election of a Republican governor in such rapidly industrializing and increasingly urban states as Florida and Texas."[2]

This prediction did come true for the South in general. The Republican revolution did occur in the sixties; however, it came in only one of the "rapidly industrializing" states—Florida—and even then the revolt proved short-lived. In 1966 Florida elected Claude R. Kirk, Jr., as its first (and to 1980 its only) Republican governor. Texas, which was the other state mentioned, did not elect a Republican in the sixties but waited until the last election of the seventies when William P. Clements became the first Republican governor in this century. Thus, only one of the two expected states followed its predicted pattern.

On the other hand, rural Arkansas, which did not seem a likely spot for the start of the Republican revolution, came up with a Republican, Winthrop Rockefeller, in 1966 for the first of his successive two-year terms. To date this election appears to have been more Rockefeller than Republican since no Republicans were elected in the seventies in Arkansas. However, the big surprise for the sixties was Virginia. The Old Dominion started electing Republicans with the last election (1969) of that decade and has continued to do so every four years since. My only defense is that Mills E. Godwin, Jr., who had first been elected as a Democrat in the sixties, turned up as the successful Republican candidate in the election of 1973. Thus, he is the only governor in the last twenty years who was elected as the candidate of both of the major parties. Godwin's switch is an interesting footnote to the political history of the governorship. However, it is hardly an excuse for missing the greatest upsurge in gubernatorial Republicanism in the South in the seventies.

Surprises such as Virginia make one wary of talking about the political pattern that may emerge in the eighties. This tendency toward caution is enhanced by an examination of Tables 2–4, which give the indices of party control for each state on a decade-by-decade basis. For example, a study of Table 4 reveals that during the 1970s there were ten states that could be called one-party Democratic. These states, mostly in the South and Southwest, are states in which the Democratic party controlled both the governorship and both houses of the legislature for the entire period 1971–80. In addition, there were seventeen normally Democratic states, seventeen two-party states, four normally Republican states, and no one-party Republican states.

A look at the one-party states over the last three decades reveals that only Alabama, Georgia, and Mississippi can be considered hard-core one-party states. Only these three states remained loyal to the Democratic party during the entire thirty-year period; all the rest strayed from the fold at one time or another, primarily in the sixties. For example, in the fifties some thirteen states could be legitimately classified as one-party Democratic. However, in the following ten-year period there were six states—Arkansas, Florida, Kentucky, Oklahoma, Tennessee, and Virginia—that elected a Republican governor and consequently dropped out of the one-party classification. Three of these—Arkansas, Florida, and Oklahoma—returned to the fold during 1971–80 but three new states—Missouri, North Carolina, and South Carolina—fell from grace by electing one or more Republican governors. The most recent defections are Texas in 1978 and Louisiana in 1979 which, after almost 100 years as solidly Democratic states, became "normally Democratic" for the last two years of the decade as a result of a Republican being elected governor.

This game of musical chairs is confusing. Politics at the state level is not a simple matter, and predictions about it are foolhardy at best and simpleminded at worst. Nevertheless, we should not be surprised to see at least one Republican elected governor in any one of the solidly Democratic states in the 1980s. Whether this gubernatorial success will presage a real party shift as it apparently has in Virginia remains to be seen. However, it is doubtful that a real shift, including securing a reasonable representation in the legislature, will occur in the remaining one-party Democratic states in the eighties. The closer one gets to the grass roots in state politics, the more difficult party shifts become because the party fights hundreds of individual battles for the legislature but only one for the governorship.

For example, Alabama in 1980 not only voted for Ronald Reagan for president but also elected its first Republican (Jeremiah Denton) to the United States Senate since Reconstruction. However, only three years earlier Fob James had felt it necessary to switch from the Republican party to the Democratic party before he subsequently launched his successful campaign for governor in 1978. In that same election, however, the Alabama voters elected a senate composed of 35 Democrats and no Republicans and a house which had 4 Republicans out of 105 members. Thus, the "Heart of Dixie" can hardly be said to be a roaring hotbed of Republicanism. However, it is rapidly becoming a more conservative state on fiscal as well as racial matters, and it is in this area of Republican philosophy that the hope for gubernatorial Republicanism lies. If George Wallace decides to run again in 1982, as is rumored at this writing, all bets are off on the election of a Republican governor in Alabama. Wallace's personal appeal and his anti-government stance would make him an almost impossible candidate for a Republican to beat.

What will happen in the normally Democratic states, the two-party states, and the normally Republican states is difficult to predict except to say that individual states will continue to shift from one category to the next as witnessed by the general trend over the last thirty years. This trend may be summarized as follows: (1) The one-party Democratic states have moved in and out of the normally Democratic category, with only three hard-core states remaining consistently Democratic throughout the period; (2) At the other end of the scale, the one-party Republican states not only have moved out of that category into the normally Republican group but have generally come to rest in the two-party classification; and (3) Some normally Democratic states have shifted to the two-party group where they have been joined by several fugitives from the old one-party Republican clan.

As things shaped up in the 1970s, the Democrats, both the one-party Democratic states and the normally Democratic states, were the gainers with twenty-seven states to the Republicans' four states. The two-party group has also picked up about five states from both ends of the spectrum to total seventeen states by 1980. This Democratic trend is expected to continue in spite of the Reagan landslide but a firm prediction is far too risky. Certainly, nothing should be projected from Tables 2–4 about individual states. It must be remembered that in the 1970s the one-party Democratic states were reduced to only three hard-core faithful—Alabama, Georgia, and Mississippi—largely because of defections in gubernatorial elections in the late 1960s. Three of six who defected in the 1960s were back in the fold for the 1970s, but it is instructive to follow the peregrinations of those who did not return. For example, Virginia, after being solidly Democratic at the state level since Reconstruction, moved out of that category in 1969 and has yet to return. During the entire period (1971–80) the Republicans controlled the governorship, but the Democrats controlled both the house and the senate. Consequently, using the formula explained in Chapter 1, the score for each year in this period in which such a political division existed would be 2.00. Since all ten years of the 1971–80 decade followed this same pattern, Virginia is ranked as 2.00 for the decade in Table 4. This ranking, based on party control of the governorship and the legislature, places the Old Dominion squarely in the mid-range of the two-party states.

The Virginia story also emphasizes the dangers of predicting the party pattern over time for any single state. Unlike most of its one-party contemporaries in the fifties and sixties, Virginia did not return to the Democratic fold after electing only one Republican. Consequently, it skipped entirely the normally Democratic stage and moved directly from one-party Democratic to genuine two-party status. Indeed, at least one observer now feels that it is two-party leaning Republican.[3] However, two-party status seems more realistic until the Republicans take over at least one house of the general assembly.

Another example, this time from the Republican side, would be North Dakota. This long-time Republican state moved from being one-party Republican during 1951–60 to two-party status in both

1961–70 and 1971–80. In the latter decade it had a Democratic governor for the entire period, a Republican senate for the entire period, and a Republican house for eight of the ten years. Therefore, it rated a 1.95 which is very close to Virginia's 2.00. However, the political pattern was the opposite of Virginia's. North Dakota had, except for two years with an even split in the house, a Democratic governor and a Republican legislature.

Writing in the 1950s, I certainly did not foresee the pattern that developed in Virginia, much less that in North Dakota, nor the complete elimination of the Republican one-party category in the 1970s. Consequently, even with the advantage of hindsight, I am loath to make a prediction for any individual state as to its probable position in the shifting tides of political fortune at the state level.

Divided Government

As demonstrated in Chapter 1, there is no fixed percentage of seats in the legislative body occupied by members of his party that guarantees the governor working control of the legislature. In fact, there can be too much of a good thing. A governor who has a very large majority of his party in the legislature generally has difficulty with that body because he does not have enough opposition members to keep his own party in line. Nevertheless, having a majority whether large or small does give the governor the advantage of having his party organize the legislature. In normal circumstances this means that the governor, through his party, can have some influence on who is selected to be speaker of the house and the chairmen of important committees. Thus, the way should be paved for smooth sailing for the governor's administration bills.

On the other hand, because of the changing political pattern discussed in the preceding section, the governor of a great many states is quite likely to find himself with too many seats controlled by his party in the legislature. This is true of all the one-party Democratic states and is generally true in the normally Democratic states. What the governor needs is enough votes to get his legislation passed, not an excess number of votes. Consequently, what actually happens in executive-legislative relations is that the governor must build up a block of votes sufficient to secure the passage of his administration bills. These votes may come either from his own party or from a combination of his own party and members of the opposition party. These opposition party members may have a philosophical compatibility with the governor, or they may have been persuaded to vote with the governor by many methods, including the judicious use of patronage. What he needs is at least one more vote than his opponents have. This one vote may well come from the opposition rather than from his own party. Since divided government has increased in the 1970s to the point where it occurs in about one-half of the states at any given legislative session, the governor may expect more than normal difficulty in getting his legislation passed. It does not, however, mean that in one-half of the states the policy-making process has come to a halt. The contemporary governor seems to struggle along in spite of what should be a stalemate between these two branches.

If we continue to have a situation of divided government, and it seems likely that we will, then the governor must look to the opposition for votes. He can do this through patronage, through the budget power, or perhaps even through philosophical compatibility. This last factor was well illustrated in the case of Virginia where a Republican governor was able to attract enough votes from conservative Democrats to get his bills passed. To be sure, this was a very unusual Republican governor, Mills Godwin, who had previously been elected as a conservative Democrat, but the principle is still the same. In Virginia the Republicans generally came from the urban areas and did not support the governor, whereas the Democrats from many of the rural areas did support him. The pattern in Virginia is repeated in slightly different versions in many states. When the governor's party is in the minority or has too great a majority, he cannot always look to his party for support but must build up a block of votes wherever he can find them. In my opinion this will be the significant executive-legislative pattern of the future; it already became a reality in many states in the 1970s. The two-party system at the state level certainly appears to have grown on paper, as was noted in Chapter 1. However, in terms of actual party control of the legislature and the governorship, there seems to be emerging a system based more on philosophical compatibility, the use of patronage, and the governor's budget powers than on appeals to party loyalty. In the 1980s there will be fewer and fewer states in which the governor will be able to call upon the members of his party in the legislature with the expectation of securing their votes on administration measures.

An Increase in Tenure Potential

As was pointed out in Chapter 1, the tenure potential of the governor has increased markedly over the last thirty years. As late as 1952 only twenty-eight states had a four-year term and only fifteen states in this group permitted the governor to succeed himself. However, by 1980 some forty-six states had a four-year term and in all but five of these he could succeed himself for at least one term. Furthermore, in eighteen of them he could succeed himself in office as long as he was able to secure reelection. This is a significant shift in the governor's tenure potential. So far, the studies that have been made indicate that the governor is partially living up to this potential. The time actually served in office increased from the 1950s to the 1960s and reached an all-time high in the 1970s when 37 percent of the governors served five years or more.[4] It seems logical to assume that this percentage will increase in the 1980s if the trend to a four-year term with no bar to immediate succession continues. While it is true that an incumbent governor is not assured of his reelection, the percentage of incumbents who were reelected in the seventies was impressive. Those incumbent governors who were permitted to run for immediate succession in the 1970s and took this option generally were successful. Of the seventy-eight incumbents who ran fifty-eight, or 74 percent, won reelection.[5]

What the governor's increased tenure potential will mean in the eighties is not entirely clear. However, it would seem that the four-year term with no bar to succession, rapidly becoming the standard pattern in the United States, should give the governor a boost in his role in policy formation. The governor needs to stay in office for more than four years primarily so that he can build a legislative bloc to support his program. His power is generally at its height during the first legislative session but tends to go downhill in subsequent sessions in those states in which the governor cannot succeed himself. However, if there is a strong possibility that the governor may succeed himself, legislators tend to pay more attention to the governor's program and to be more receptive to his viewpoint. After all, a governor who can affect a legislator's constituency for an eight-year period is of more consequence than a chief executive who can affect it for only a four-year period.

The governor's role in management also should be strengthened by this extended term. It is very difficult for a governor coming into office to get a clear picture of the management problems of the state in less than one or two years. In fact, several of the governors who commented on this point felt that it took at least a four-year term for the governor to become familiar enough with administrative operations to have much of an influence on it even though he might have an extensive appointive power. If this is true, it seems desirable for the governor to have a second term, provided of course that the electorate supports his policies, so that he will be able to influence policy not only through legislation but also through the executive branch. It should be of great assistance to the governor to have his own men in office over a number of years and would assist in what is euphemistically known as the coordination of the executive branch. What this phrase means in practice is that the governor's policies do not disappear when they leave his office but are actually carried out and, when necessary, coordinated with other agencies. When all these agencies are under the control of a governor for a period of eight years, some real progress can be made on the administrative front. The shorter the governor's term, the more he is regarded as a bird of passage by old-line administrators. They have seen other governors come and go and only give lip service to the current governor, particularly if they feel they will have to put up with him for only four years.

While all of this conjecture is highly unscientific, it seems to have considerable basis in practical politics. Consequently, the governor's powers seem to have been enhanced both by extension of his term and by the possibility that the governor can succeed himself. When a governor takes office, he inherits most of the budget of the outgoing governor because of a lack of time to make any extensive changes. Not until the second budget does the governor get any of his real policies into operation and, if he has only a four-year term, his influence tends to be downhill after that. Thus, to predict for the eighties, it would appear that the increase in the governor's tenure potential will prove significant in strengthening the American governorship vis-à-vis not only the legislative but also the executive branch of government.

The Rising Cost of Campaigning

Chapter 2 documented in some detail two closely related developments in regard to gubernatorial campaigning in the 1970s. The first of these was that the cost of campaigning has skyrocketed in the last ten years. The rapidly increasing cost of running for the state's highest office raises at least one important question about the election process in a democracy. This question is how campaigning may be brought within the reach of any qualified citizen so that the race for governor will not be restricted only to candidates of great personal wealth.

The second major point made in the chapter was that the technology of gubernatorial campaigning has changed appreciably since the 1950s. In the 1970s a successful candidate had to hire a political consultant or a public relations firm specializing in the management of political campaigns. The candidate also had to make extensive use of television, which has come to be decisive in the gubernatorial popularity contest. When the cost of a political consultant and the sums spent for television are added to the cost of traditional campaign techniques, they make almost any gubernatorial campaign prohibitively expensive. In addition, the new technology produces a campaign in which the outcome appears to turn more on the proper packaging of the candidate and less on the issues than even the campaigns of the fifties, which were never noted for comprehensive discussions of the major problems facing the state.

The analysis in Chapter 2 clearly shows that the cost of running for governor has increased rapidly in the last ten years if judged by the actual dollars which a candidate must spend in order to be elected. In addition, the cost of campaigning has increased on the cost per vote cast for the winning candidate, and even for the losing candidate in most elections. Thus, it is reasonable to conclude that, based on the usually accepted measuring devices for election costs, it costs more to run for governor in the 1970s than it did in the 1950s. Of course, there are some campaigns, such as those recently conducted in West Virginia and Tennessee, where the presence of men of great personal wealth made the campaign expenditures of both the winner and the loser seem almost incredible when compared to the size of the state and the size of the electorate. Also, there are special situations, as was the case in Alaska in 1980, where the total expenditures were not nearly as high as in some of the "lower forty-eight" states but the small population and low turnout of voters made the cost per vote extremely high and perhaps atypical even for the 1970s.

Neither of these situations, the rich man's race or the unusual area-population ratio in Alaska, suggests that the cost of running for governor is decreasing. Rather they are special cases where the cost is higher than normal due to the presence of certain factors peculiar to the race or to the state.

On the other hand, there are at least two studies of the cost of campaigning which suggest that, on a relative basis, the cost of gubernatorial campaigns is decreasing rather than increasing. These two studies certainly should be noted before concluding a brief recapitulation of what seems to be a serious problem in democratic governance at the state level.

The first study analyzed the expenditures in the gubernatorial campaigns in Florida from 1960 through 1978. The methodology used differed from that used in this book since the Florida study was concerned with the total expenditures of all candidates spending over $10,000 in the election. For example, there were eight candidates in 1960 who spent a total of $2.2 million while in 1978 there were also eight candidates but this group spent $10.3 million. In the six elections covered, the spending of all major candidates for governor was as follows: 1960—$2.2 million; 1964—$3.2 million; 1966—$3.4 million; 1970—$3.1 million; 1974—$1.4 million; and 1978—$10.3 million. It is clear from these figures that the upward trend in the expenditure pattern did not always run in a straight line. For example, in 1966 spending reached a peak that was not surpassed until 1978. The explanation for this aberration was that in 1966 the Republicans went all out to win the governorship, but their success was expensive. On the other hand, in 1974 there was an unusually small expenditure. In this election a popular incumbent, Governor Ruben Askew, did not have to mount much of a campaign to defeat his opponents. The reverse was true in 1978 when Askew was out of the race and there were wide open and very expensive Republican as well as Democratic primaries, plus a general election in which the Republican candidate was supposed to have a real chance of winning the governorship. The result was a $10 million campaign that was the high for the six elections analyzed.[6]

So far none of these data (except those for 1974) really contradict the general proposition that it was more costly to run for governor in the 1970s than in the 1960s. However, the authors of the Florida study feel that some weight should be given to the increasing population of a state in computing gubernatorial costs. In a rapidly growing state like Florida "what seems to be happening is that while per candidate expenditures for the top candidates are increasing consistently, the population of Florida is increasing at such a more rapid pace that the per candidate per citizen expenditures seem to be decreasing."[7] Their analysis also attempts to compensate for the Consumer Price Index increases by changing all expenditures to a standardized total campaign expenditure based on 1980 as 100 percent. This device changes the expenditure totals; for example the expenditures for 1960 become $5.6 million and those for 1978 become $11.7 million. However, the relative expenditures do not change and the conclusion cited above is based in a trend line which reflects these "standardized" expenditures.

A similar study has been made by the California Fair Political Practices Commission. This analysis shows that both in actual dollars or in constant dollars (in this case 1958 dollars), the cost of running for governor in California follows a fluctuating pattern similar to that in Florida. The California figures, in terms of actual dollars, are: 1958—$2.7 million; 1962—$4.5 million; 1966—$6.9 million; 1970—$4.9 million; 1974—$10.6 million; and 1978—$13.5 million. In commenting on this study, Herbert Alexander states that "The study revealed that while California campaign costs are increasing in terms of actual dollars, once inflation is factored out, the cost of gubernatorial campaigning has remained relatively unchanged over the last 20 years when expressed in terms of constant

1958 dollars.''[8] This finding, while encouraging as an abstract proposition, is small consolation to prospective candidates for governor in California. Even if inflation is factored out, the 1974 election cost the principal candidates $6.3 million in 1958 dollars, and the 1978 election cost an actual $13.5 million even though it was only $5.8 million in 1958 dollars. It seems probable, although this was not a part of the California study, that if the campaign costs in California were "corrected" for population, they would show a pattern similar to that in Florida. California is a rapidly growing state and should show the Florida pattern of decreased cost per inhabitant.

These two studies are extremely interesting although we will not know if their findings are representative of all states until we have additional studies which confirm or cast doubt on the conclusions reached. One factor that may make a difference if these studies are replicated in other states is that both California and Florida have populations which are growing faster than those in the average state. Consequently, the findings in the Florida study of a decreasing cost per citizen in gubernatorial campaigning might well apply to California. It probably will apply to other Sun Belt states with rapidly growing populations. However, it seems doubtful that it will apply to those states with stable or relatively decreasing populations. The rise in population in Alabama, for example, was only enough between 1970 and 1980 to keep that state at the median of population growth. Hence it is unlikely that the cost per candidate per citizen will have decreased over the period 1970–80. As the Florida study suggests, if the cost is to decrease, the population must be growing more rapidly than the cost of campaigning. Inflation has been hitting campaign costs about as hard as any other activity. In addition, television and other technological costs have substantially increased the cost of the modern campaign. Consequently, the cost per citizen per candidate should not be expected to decrease in most states. In fact, over the period 1970–80 the cost per citizen should increase. This has been true of the cost per voter in all the states for which cost data were available in Chapter 2. It is even true in the case of Florida in terms of actual dollars. For example, the 1978 gubernatorial election in Florida was not only the most expensive in the state's history in terms of the total amount spent but it was also the most expensive in terms of the cost per vote cast. The turnout, some 4.8 million voters, was the largest in the state's history, but the total cost of over $10.3 million also was the largest expenditure ever. Even the large turnout did not balance the expenditures. As a consequence it cost $2.13 per vote cast. Prior to the 1978 election the most expensive election in the state had been in 1966 when a push by the Republicans resulted in an expenditure of $3.1 million but a cost of only about $0.89 per vote cast.

As interesting as these speculations about the cost of campaigning relative to population and inflation may be, they are not the primary concern of this book. Neither the California nor the Florida study is directed to the question of what it will cost an aspiring gubernatorial candidate to run for the state's highest office in one of these states. This is the primary focus of Chapter 2 of this study. Since we are concerned with what it cost to become governor in the personal sense of the cost to the candidate, the overall totals are not of as much significance for our purposes.

On the other hand, the focus of this book in regard to the cost of elections and the data from these two studies do come together at one critical juncture. This juncture is at the point when we focus on the implication of the cost of becoming governor for the process of democratic governance. In discussing this problem, it really does not make very much difference whether the question is approached from the perspective of an individual candidate or from the point of view of the total cost of the election. The problem is the same in each case—namely that it costs so much to become the governor of any state that it has become a matter of grave public concern. Where can the "poor but honest candidate," so beloved in American political folklore, expect to find the one, two or three million dollars which he will need to have a reasonable chance of being elected governor? One answer, with all of its well understood ramifications, is from interest groups of one kind or another. They may be power companies pushing nuclear power plants or anti-nuclear environmentalists pushing a return to an agrarian society. From the point of view of democratic government, both groups have a right to be heard and to participate in the political process. Whether the general public is well served by having a governor who was bought by either is the question at hand. If the answer is that it is not in the public interest, then someone must come up with the plan for a better political mousetrap. Some seventeen legislatures with seventeen plans think they have the solution, various forms of public financing. Critics of public financing already charge that the system as constituted in most states gives an advantage to the imcumbent; other critics decry the undesirable side effects of the restriction of freedom that comes with the limits on expenditures in these plans. However, the critics have not suggested a viable alternative. The better gubernatorial mousetrap is still to be built. It is a challenge in practical politics that remains to be solved in the 1980s.

Gubernatorial Functions: A Shift in Emphasis

There were two principal questions to be answered by this study in regard to the governor's functions. First, did the study reveal that the governors in the seventies had the same basic functions as the governors of the fifties? Second, did the governors in the seventies place the same degree of emphasis on the various aspects of their functions as did their counterparts some twenty years earlier? A short answer is "yes" to the first question and "no" to the second. The findings of this study show that the governors of the seventies still have the same three primary functions as the governors of the fifties, namely policy formation, public relations, and management. On the other hand, the study shows that the relative emphasis placed on these functions is different in the seventies from that found in the fifties. The primary function of the governor still remains that of policy formation, and the most time-consuming continues to be public relations. However, in the twenty-year period there has been a growing emphasis placed on management, both in terms of the amount of time devoted to it by the governors and the importance given to it in their own views of their functions. Both of these findings are documented at some length in Chapter 3. However, it may be well to review briefly the evidence supporting both conclusions.

The comparison of demands on the governor's time both in the 1950s and 1970s clearly showed that public relations was the most time-consuming of the governor's functions. An analysis of his weekly schedule in 1949 showed that the governor of New Hampshire devoted about 26.6 percent of his time to such public relations functions as press conferences, preparing and giving speeches, christening a naval vessel, bill-signing ceremonies, meeting with schoolchildren, and acting as an honored guest at various functions. Actually he may have spent more time on public relations since some of the 15 percent of the time spent on correspondence and a part of the 6 percent of the time spent on the telephone probably were devoted to public relations.

In the 1970s the pattern was almost exactly the same for the governor of Illinois, who spent 27 percent of his time in 1971 on public relations as opposed to 19 percent on management. In both cases public relations was the single most time-consuming function. Management came in second in Illinois as it did in New Hampshire where it occupied about 21 percent of the governor's time. However, Governor Sherman Adams of New Hampshire had an unusually strong interest in administration. For example, in the weeks studied he devoted some time to an employee reclassification study and to a state reorganization. His 21 percent devoted to administration probably was high for the 1950s.

A broader study in 1978, which covered forty states, calculated management at 29 percent. On the other hand, the time spent on public relations functions such as meeting the general public (14 percent), ceremonial functions (14 percent), and working with the press and media (9 percent) added up to 37 percent. A comparison of different studies with different definitions of such functions as public relations and management is difficult, and the results are probably not too accurate.

In all the cases studied in both the fifties and the seventies the function to which the governor devoted the most time was public relations and the second was the management of the state government. The third function in terms of time was policy formation although few of the studies used this term. It is concealed under such headings as "working with the federal government," "working with the legislature," "miscellaneous," "legislative relations," "political leadership," and a host of other euphemisms. However, it was my considered judgment that even though policy formation was probably only third in time devoted to it, the function, nevertheless, was the most important of the governor's functions. The reasons for this belief are spelled out in considerable detail in both Chapter 3 on "The Executive Function" and Chapter 4 on "The Governor's Role in Policy Formation."

Most governors continued to place a heavy emphasis on policy formation in the 1970s. However, the emphasis on management in the 1970s definitely was greater than that in the 1950s. On the other hand, when the views of the governors on the duties which they found to be the most difficult were examined, as was done in Chapter 3, they did not list management as one of the functions which they considered difficult. The two aspects of their duties most frequently mentioned in this category were interference with family life and working with the legislature. The "management of state government" was ranked last by the governors in a list of eleven different aspects of the office. However, this ranking does not mean that the function is unimportant—only that the governors found it less difficult than their other duties.

If the evidence presented in Chapter 3 is taken as a whole, the increasing salience of management in the 1970s emerges. It does not yet replace public relations in terms of time consumed nor does it replace policy formation in importance. While it is interesting to speculate on the possibility of the governor becoming primarily the state's "general manager" in the 1980s, I do not expect this shift in functions to occur.

The eighties would appear to be a decade of difficult economic problems. In the short run, these probably will take the form of inflation and recession. In the long run they may be more localized with a number of the industrial states hard hit by foreign competition in everything from steel to stereos. Consequently, there will be an increasing need for leadership at the state level to solve not only the economic but also the social problems that are sure to accompany severe economic dislocation. The governors should rise to the challenge of the eighties in providing this leadership. Consequently, for the eighties as for the seventies the governor should continue to operate as the state's leader in the formation of public policy.

Notes

1. Coleman B. Ransone, Jr., "Political Leadership in the Governor's Office," *Journal of Politics* 26 (February 1964): 197–220.

2. Ibid., p. 219.

3. Larry Sabato, *Goodbye to Good-Time Charlie: The American Governor Transformed, 1950–1975* (Lexington, Mass.: D.C. Heath, 1978), p. 139.

4. Sarah McCally Morehouse, *State Politics, Parties and Policy* (New York: Holt, Rinehart and Winston, 1980), p. 206.

5. Ibid., p. 207.

6. Douglas St. Angelo, Annie Mary Hartsfield, and William Ruefle, *Campaign Finance in Florida* (Tallahassee, Florida: Institute for Social Research, Florida State University, 1980), pp. 12–15. Additional data furnished in letters from William Ruefle dated 7 May 1980 and 25 September 1980.

7. St. Angelo, Hartsfield and Ruefle, *Campaign Finance in Florida,* p. 16.

8. California Fair Political Practices Commission, *Campaign Costs: How Much They Have Increased and Why: A Study of State Elections, 1958–1978* (Sacramento, Calif.: California Fair Political Practices Commission, 1980), cited in Herbert E. Alexander, "Financing Gubernatorial Election Campaigns," *State Government* 53 (Summer 1980): 142.

SELECTED BIBLIOGRAPHY

Books and Monographs

Bollens, John C. and Williams, G. Robert. *Jerry Brown in a Plain Brown Wrapper*. Pacific Palisades, Calif.: Palisades Publishers, 1978.

California Fair Political Practices Commission. *Campaign Costs: How Much They Have Increased and Why: A Study of State Elections, 1958-1978*. Sacramento, Calif.: California Fair Political Practices Commission, 1980.

Carter, Jimmy. *Why Not the Best?* Nashville, Tenn.: Broadman Press, 1975.

Center for Policy Research. *Governing the American States: A Handbook for New Governors*. Washington, D.C.: National Governors' Association, 1978.

Coffman, Tom. *Catch A Wave: A Case Study of Hawaii's New Politics*. Honolulu: The University Press of Hawaii, 1973.

Council of State Governments. *The Book of the States*. Lexington, Ky.: Council of State Governments, published biennially.

Farmer, Hallie. *The Legislative Process in Alabama*. University, Ala.: Bureau of Public Administration, 1949.

Halley, Willis D. *Should California Pocket the "Pocket Veto"?* Berkeley, Calif.: Institute of Governmental Studies, 1966.

Keefe, William J. and Ogul, Morris S. *The American Legislative Process: Congress and the States*. 4th ed. Englewood Cliffs, New Jersey: Prentice-Hall, 1977.

Kirkpatrick, James C. *The Annual Statistical Report of Expenditures Made in Connection with the 1976 Elections*. Missouri: 12 May 1977.

Morehouse, Sarah McCally. *State Politics, Parties and Policy*. New York: Holt, Rinehart and Winston, 1980.

New Jersey Election Law Enforcement Commission. *Public Financing in New Jersey: The 1977 General Election for Governor*. Trenton, N.J., 1978.

Pack, Robert. *Jerry Brown: The Philosopher-Prince*. New York: Stein and Day, 1978.

Public Affairs Research Council of Louisiana, *PAR Analysis: The Great Louisiana Campaign Spendathon,* pamphlet no. 243 (March 1980).

Ransone, Coleman B., Jr. *The Office of Governor in the South*. University: University of Alabama Press, 1951.

–––––. *The Office of Governor in the United States*. University: University of Alabama Press, 1956.

Sabato, Larry. *Aftermath of "Armageddon": An Analysis of the 1973 Virginia Gubernatorial Election*. Charlottesville: Institute of Government, University of Virginia, 1975.

–––––. *Goodbye to Good-Time Charlie: The American Governor Transformed, 1950–1975*. Lexington, Mass.: D.C. Heath, 1978.

St. Angelo, Douglas; Hartsfield, Annie May; and Ruefle, William. *Campaign Finance in Florida*. Tallahassee: Institute for Social Research, Florida State University, 1980.

Weinberg, Martha Wagner. *Managing the State*. Cambridge, Mass.: MIT Press, 1972.

Articles

Alexander, Herbert E. "Financing Gubernatorial Election Campaigns." *State Government* 53 (Summer 1980): 140–43.

Austin, Robert J. "The 1978–79 Virginia Assembly: End of a Decade." *University of Virginia Newsletter* 55 (September 1979): 1–4.

Bernick, E. Lee. "Gubernatorial Tools: Formal vs. Informal." *Journal of Politics* 41 (May 1979): 656–64.

Beyle, Thad L. "Governors' Views on Being Governor." *State Government* 52 (Summer 1979): 103–9.

Cook, Rhodes and West, Stacy. "1978 Gubernatorial Contests: Incumbent Winners Hold Money Advantage." *Congressional Quarterly Weekly Report,* 25 August 1979, pp. 1755–56.

Gwyn, Robert J. "The Power of the Press: Broadcast Media." *Popular Government* [University of North Carolina] 44 (Fall 1978): 6–9.

Hall-Sizemore, Richard W. "Money in Politics: Financing the 1977 Statewide Elections in Virginia." *University of Virginia Newsletter* 56 (August 1980): 45–50.

Loomis, Kenneth. "Legislators Explain Nunn's Fiscal Arm-Twisting." *Louisville* (Ky.) *Courier Journal,* 7 March 1968, sec. B, p. 4.

McCally [Morehouse], Sarah. "The Governor and His Legislative Party." *American Political Science Review* 60 (December 1966): 933–41.

Mendelsohn, Ethel and Galvin, John H. "The Legal Status of Women." In *The Book of the States, 1978–79.* Lexington, Kentucky: Council of State Governments, 1978.

Morehouse, Sarah McCally. "The State Political Party and the Policy-Making Process." *American Political Science Review* 67 (March 1973): 55–72.

Prescott, Frank W. "The Executive Veto in American States." *Western Political Quarterly* 3 (March 1950): 97–111.

———. "The Executive Veto in Southern States." *Journal of Politics* 10 (November 1948): 659–75.

Quinn, Tony. "Political Action Committees—The New Campaign Bank-rollers." *California Journal,* March 1979, pp. 36–38.

Ransone, Coleman B., Jr. "Political Leadership in the Governor's Office." *Journal of Politics* 26 (February 1964): 197–220.

———, ed. "The American Governor in the 1970s." A Symposium. *Public Administration Review* 30 (January/February 1970): 1–42.

Sharkansky, Ira. "Agency Requests, Gubernatorial Support and Budget Success in State Legislatures." *American Political Science Review* 62 (December 1968): 1220–31.

Steif, William. "Big Cities Dependency on U.S. Growing." *Birmingham* (Ala.) *Post Herald,* 27 March 1978, sec. A, p. 6.

Stevenson, Tommy. "He's a Politician without the Election." *Tuscaloosa* (Ala.) *News,* 27 August 1978, sec. D, p. 3.

"Survey on State Campaign Finance." *Comparative State Politics Newsletter* [University of Kentucky] 1 (January 1980): 22–23.

Walker, Alexander J. "The Governor's Veto Power." *University of Virginia Newsletter* 55 (December 1977): 13–16.

Walker, David B. and Richter, Albert J. "States and the Impact of Federal Grants." *State Government* 50 (Spring 1977): 83–88.

Wyner, Alan S. "Gubernatorial Relations with Legislators and Administrators." *State Government* 41 (Summer 1968): 199–203.

Selected Interviews

Anderson, Sigurd. Republican Governor of South Dakota, 1951–55. In Pierre, South Dakota, 10 July 1951.

Anselmi, Rudolph. Former long-time legislator and now Chairman, Wyoming Commission on Revenue and Taxation. In Cheyenne, Wyoming, 7 December 1976.

Apodaca, Jerry. Democratic Governor of New Mexico 1975–79. In Santa Fe, New Mexico, 16 December 1976.

Barren, Joan. Reporter for the *Wyoming State Tribune*. In Cheyenne, Wyoming, 6 December 1976.

Barth, Bob. Reporter, KVSF News. In Santa Fe, New Mexico, 16 December 1976.

Brown, David R. Executive Assistant to Governor Milton J. Shapp. In Harrisburg, Pennsylvania, 19 November 1976.

Brown, Vincent. Clerk of the Legislature. In Lincoln, Nebraska, 2 December 1976.

Bruhn, William. Director of Intergovernmental Relations on the staff of Governor Calvin L. Rampton. In Salt Lake City, Utah, 8 December 1976.

Byars, Robert S. Director of Research, Arizona Office of Economic Planning and Development. In Phoenix, Arizona, 14 December 1976.

Castro, Raul H. Democratic Governor of Arizona 1975–77. In Phoenix, Arizona, 11 December 1976.

Clapp, Kenyon. Executive Assistant to Governor Dolph Briscoe. In Austin, Texas, 17 December 1976.

Cochran, Chan. Administrative Assistant to Governor James A. Rhodes. In Columbus, Ohio, 22 November 1976.

Coleman, Elizabeth. Press Secretary to Governor Edmund G. Brown, Jr. In Sacramento, California, 9 December 1976.

DeConcini, Dino. Chief Executive Assistant to Governor Raul H.Castro. In Phoenix, Arizona, 13 December 1976.

Dougherty, Anthony. Legislative Assistant to Governor Edmund G. Brown, Jr. In Sacramento, California, 11 December 1976.

Fauliso, Joseph J. President Pro Tem of the Senate, Connecticut General Assembly. In Hartford, Connecticut, 15 November 1976.

Foote, David. Executive Director of the Human Services Cabinet, Office of Governor Richard D. Lamm. In Denver, Colorado, 3 December 1976.

Gunther, C.L. Deputy Majority Leader, Connecticut House of Representavies. In Hartford, Connecticut, 16 November 1976.

Hillard, Carl. Reporter for the Associated Press. In Denver, Colorado, 3 December 1976.

Humphreys, Hugh. Administrative Assistant to Governor Richard D. Lamm. In Denver, Colorado, 2 December 1976.

Ingram, Carl. Reporter, United Press International. In Sacramento, California, 10 December 1976.

Jacobson, John D. Director of the Budget, State of Nebraska. In Lincoln, Nebraska, 2 December 1976.

Johnson, David A. Director, Legislative Services Commission, State of Ohio. In Columbus, Ohio, 22 November 1976.

Johnson, David. Reporter, *Salt Lake City Tribune.* In Salt Lake City, Utah, 9 December 1976.

Kennedy, Thomas C. Senator in the Nebraska unicameral legislature. In Lincoln, Nebraska, 1 December 1976.

Krupsak, Mary Anne. Lieutenant Governor, State of New York. Telephone interview in Albany, New York, 16 November 1976.

Leonard, Brad. Director of the Executive Budget, State of Colorado. In Denver, Colorado, 3 December 1976.

Lewinsohn, Nancy. Executive Aide to Governor Ella Grasso. In Hartford, Connecticut, 15 November 1976.

McCollam, Chad. Legislative Liaison for Governor Ella Grasso. In Hartford, Connecticut, 15 November 1976.

Mahoney, Jerry. Press Secretary to Governor Ed Herschler. In Cheyenne, Wyoming, 6 December 1976.

Meshel, Harry. Senator and Majority Whip of the Ohio Senate. In Columbus, Ohio, 23 November 1976.

Miller, Carl. Press Secretary to Governor Richard D. Lamm. In Denver, Colorado, 2 December 1976.

Miller, Michael. Executive Assistant to Governor Calvin L. Rampton. In Salt Lake City, Utah, 8 December 1976.

Millican, Michael W. State House Correspondent for the Associated Press. In Hartford, Connecticut, 16 November 1976.

Montoya, Vincent J. Director of Finance and Administration, State of New Mexico. In Santa Fe, New Mexico, 15 December 1976.

O'Donnel, Harry J. Director of Communications, Executive Chamber, State of New York. In Albany, New York, 18 November 1976.

Otto, Norman A. Administrative Assistant to Governor J. James Exon. In Lincoln, Nebraska, 1 December 1976.

Powell, Minnie Mae. Executive Secretary to Governor Raul Castro. In Phoenix, Arizona, 13 December 1976.

Schmit, Loran. Senator in the Nebraska unicameral legislature. In Lincoln, Nebraska, 1 December 1976.

Sheridan, Richard G. Legislative Budget Officer, State of Ohio. In Columbus, Ohio, 23 November 1976.

Skelton, Nancy. Reporter, *Sacramento Bee*. In Sacramento, California, 10 December 1976.

Skinner, C. Richard. Administrative Assistant to Governor Ed Herschler. In Cheyenne, Wyoming, 6 December 1976.

Slocum, Peter. Reporter for the Associated Press. In Albany, New York, 18 November 1976.

Stack, Ronald. Program Associate, Executive Chamber, State of New York. In Albany, New York, 16 November 1976.

Tepper, Jay. Connecticut Commissioner of Finance and Administration. In Hartford, Connecticut, 15 November 1976.

Thomas, Ralph. Head of Legislative Services for the Wyoming Legislature. In Cheyenne, Wyoming, 6 December 1976.

Travis, Charles D. Director, Budget and Planning, State of Texas. In Austin, Texas, 17 December 1976.

Tussy, Rodney. Reporter, *Deseret News*. In Salt Lake City, Utah, 9 December 1976.

Vickerman, John L. Chief Deputy Legislative Analyst, Legislative Budget Committee, Office of the Legislative Analyst. In Sacramento, California, 10 December 1976.

Whelan, Gerald T. Lieutenant Governor, State of Nebraska. In Lincoln, Nebraska, 2 December 1976.

Williams, Robert M. Legislative Analyst, Joint Budget Committee of the Colorado General Assembly. In Denver, Colorado, 4 December 1976.

Witt, Lee. Administrative Assistant to Governor Jerry Apodaca. In Santa Fe, New Mexico, 15 December 1976.

Works, George. Press Secretary of the Texas House of Representatives. In Austin, Texas, 17 December 1976.

Cases

Buckley v. Valeo, 424 U.S. 1 (1976).

MacMannus v. Love, Colorado, 499 P. 2d 609.

Shapp v. Sloan and the General Assembly of Pennsylvania, Pa., 391 A.2d 595.

Speeches and Panels

Caldwell, Millard F. "The Governor's Duties and Responsibilities." Address before the Thirty-First Annual Meeting of the Florida State Chamber of Commerce. St. Petersburg, Florida, 2 December 1947.

Donnell, Forrest C. "The Usual Duties of the Governor." Address before
     the National Governors' Conference, 23 June 1943, in *Proceedings
     of the Governors' Conference, 1943.*
Walker, Daniel. Remarks made as commentator on a panel on "The Con-
     temporary Governor" at the Thirty-Seventh Annual Meeting of the
     Midwest Political Science Association, Chicago, Illinois, 20 April
     1979.

INDEX

About the Author

COLEMAN B. RANSONE, JR., is Professor of Political Science at the University of Alabama. His earlier works include *The Office of Governor in the South* and *The Office of Governor in the United States.*